THE
ONE TO ONE
TOOLKIT

Tips and Strategies for Advisers, Coaches and Mentors

Careertrain Publishing

By the same Authors:

The Groupwork Toolkit: How to convert your one to one advice skills to work with groups
Ann Reynolds and Julie Cooper ISBN 978   0955968013
This book is essential for coaches and advisers who may have to work with more than one client at a time. It de-mystifies groupwork, showing you how to plan and run a successful session.

The Job Interview Toolkit: Exercises to get you fit for your interview
Ann Reynolds and Julie Cooper ISBN 978 0955968020
A practical, easy to follow guide to preparing for interviews. It contains a selection of activities, organised in the five-step TAPAS programme, designed to get you fit to perform like a star on the day. An excellent resource for advisers.

By Julie Cooper:

Face to Face in the Workplace: A Handbook of Strategies for Effective Discussions
Julie Cooper ISBN 978 0955968037
This highly acclaimed book has won praise from many sources and is rapidly becoming adopted as a key reference tool, both for busy managers and also students on business courses.

Five Steps to being Heard: How to get your message across to the right person
Julie Cooper ISBN 978 0955968099
Do you sometimes get taken for granted or overlooked? Are you always recognised for the talents you bring? If you want someone to hear your message, then this is the book for you. It will help you identify why your message isn't always being heard, and give you strategies to makes sure the people who matter hear what you have to say.

All titles are available at www.springpublishing.co.uk

THE
ONE TO ONE
TOOLKIT

Tips and Strategies for Advisers, Coaches and Mentors

Julie Cooper and
Ann Reynolds

© Copyright Julie Cooper and Ann Reynolds 2008
© Illustrations copyright Lici Cosserat 2008
First published 2008
Reprinted with amendments 2009, 2010
2nd Edition 2013

ISBN 978-0-9559680-5-1

Published by
CareerTrain
www.careertrain.net
info@careertrain.net

Printed and bound in the UK

Note: The material contained in this book is set out in good faith for general guidance only and no liability can be accepted for loss or expense incurred as a result of relying in particular circumstances on statements made in this book.

CONTENTS

FOREWORD

Is this book for you?

- Do you work one-to-one with people who need information or advice?
- As an expert in your own profession, do you advise individuals on a one-to-one basis?
- Are you an administrator or a receptionist whose job has developed into providing information and advice?

If you have a job that requires you to help move others forward in their lives and use one-to-one interaction to do this, you will probably find The One to One Toolkit a useful resource.

This book is a practical guide for people working face to face with clients, bringing together ideas we have found useful, most of which were first developed by other people. It does not claim to be an academic work offering new models or theories. In the bibliography we have provided a list of the works written by the authors we mention in the text, so if you want to read more detail, you can look them up there.

It is written principally for those whose job is in the field of "IAG" (Information, Advice and Guidance for Learning and Work), but if you work in another sector that involves giving advice or guidance, you may well find tools and techniques that will add value to your practice; in fact anyone who carries out the duties of an adviser where the focus is to meet the needs of the client, or patient, or learner, or enquirer (rather than to sell them something or persuade them to do something), can use the approaches we offer. It may well be invaluable if you have moved sideways into your role from another profession, or if your job role has changed to meet new agenda. It is aimed at those working with ordinary, or even extraordinary, people but is not in sufficient depth for those working with clients who have counselling or other therapeutic needs.

The value of supporting individuals through changes, encouraging them to reach their potential and make the best of their lives, is high on the political agenda for many reasons and this is reflected in many developments in public sector roles.

You may work for a...

- Student services centre
- Learning centre
- Advice centre
- Careers service
- "nextstep" service
- University careers service
- Connexions service
- Outplacement service
- Jobcentre
- Learning provider
- Library
- Housing Service
- Law Centre

And your professional role may be...

- Careers adviser
- Guidance practitioner
- Learning adviser
- Coach
- Mentor
- Teacher
- Lecturer
- Tutor
- Information assistant
- Librarian or library officer/assistant
- Student services adviser
- Admissions adviser

What you will all have in common is the awareness that carrying out an advice or guidance interview is not as easy as it looks. An interview that fully meets the client's needs may appear to be just a natural conversation. In fact the adviser will be multi-tasking with considerable skill.

Those of us who carry out helping interviews with clients often wonder how much use we have really been. Some of the concerns we have felt are:-

The client hardly said a word. I couldn't get him to open up and tell me what he felt.

I couldn't tell if I had given the client what she wanted.

The client seemed to lose interest and didn't really listen to me.

The client talked and talked, I couldn't get a word in, and we didn't get anything sorted out.

For everything I suggested, the client found a reason why it wouldn't work, she didn't seem to want me to find a solution.

Of course, there are many more things that worry us after a one-to-one session, for example:

- I had so much to tell the client that we ran out of time

- I offered the client a second meeting to help him further, but he didn't want it

- The client didn't do any of the things I suggested, I felt I had wasted my time

- I seem to take too long over interviews, sometimes I get lost and find it hard to keep focused

- I am so worried the client will ask me something I can't answer, that I'm reluctant to dig too deep

- I hate it when the client gets emotional, I can't handle it

- I know I talk too much, but I don't know how to deal with it

- Sometimes right at the end of the interview the client brings in a new issue which completely changes the situation

And how does it feel for the client?

Most of us can recall going to an expert for help or advice and coming away disappointed. Perhaps we felt the adviser did not seem to understand what we were asking, was not really listening to us, or that they loaded us with information but it was not what we actually needed. We did not like to complain, but felt we were wasting our time.

How this book will help you

This book will suggest ways to avoid some of these difficulties. It will give you two well used models which you can use to structure your interviews, so that you can build an open relationship with your clients at the same time as remaining focused and providing them with what they came for.

First and foremost, it is about listening; it is also about thinking and talking constructively. It will look at some of the common pitfalls, and provide hints on how to avoid them.

In addition, it provides a range of approaches and exercises to help you improve your practice and equip you to really understand your clients - and to help clients understand themselves. The tools are cross-referenced to some of the types of client we often find it difficult to help, so if you are looking for fresh ideas for dealing with a ditherer or an unrealistic client, you can flip straight to that section.

This book is far from comprehensive; there are myriad other tools, theories and models you can access in other places. What we are providing you with here is a starting point of relatively user-friendly and useful concepts to help you on your way. We hope you enjoy experimenting with some of the ideas in this book, and that it gives you food for thought, fresh ideas, and a new impetus to do your very best for all your clients.

Who are Julie and Ann?

We are independent guidance advisers and trainers based in Cambridgeshire who first met about 15 years ago working for the county's Adult Guidance Service, then went our separate ways until we met up again recently and decided to join forces to form CareerTrain.

Why we wrote this book

Ann:

My guidance career has included advising school leavers and further education students, adult guidance, setting up a consultancy offering a guidance service to employees in the workplace and training other advisers through NVQ and short interview skills courses.

The one constant throughout has been my one to one interviewing. I learned good interview practice at college, but in the heat of the job, under pressure to meet targets and people's different expectations, it's easy to lose the thread. Re-visiting the models and theories has helped me to see why and when things go wrong – did I rush in too quickly without taking the time and trouble to build rapport, did I forget to establish a clear contract, was I clear enough about my own role, did I ask the right kind of questions, did I listen, did I talk too much, did I summarise, did I give the client time to tell his story?

For the last eight years, training and assessing advisers, I've watched people go through the same interview horrors as me, but I've also learned from watching some really excellent practice. I have found it very helpful to base interviews on a model structure, in fact I often use two well established models to remind me what needs to be done and in what order. In this book I share these with you as I do with trainees, linking them to newer models now available to us, in the hope that they will help you feel more in control of the interview process and more able to keep the client at the centre of your helping.

Julie:

Jobs involving advice and guidance usually attract those of us who like to work with others, yet the paradox is that the actual role can be a lonely affair – sometimes we do outreach work and don't see colleagues all day long; even if we are based in a busy office, we can still spend the best part of the day in an interview room with a succession of clients passing through, yet no fellow advisers to hand. Ultimately, you can end up wondering if you are doing the job properly at all.

There can be too few opportunities to meet peers to exchange ideas, compare practice and support each other. I remember very lively team meetings where we hurled thoughts at each other in a none too orderly fashion - things we had found out, ideas, problems, challenging cases, solutions - such was our enthusiasm to learn from each other and improve our practice. Our manager was very good humoured in keeping us focused while giving us opportunity to vent our feelings.

When I began training advisers, I soon discovered that the same questions, fears and concerns arose time and again, and I increasingly became interested in bringing together the tools and techniques that you will find here. Some I discovered myself, some from colleagues, others from students. Logically, it seemed sensible to give a sound framework for practice in front of the tools: a solid foundation of understanding is needed before the tools can be used.

Incidentally, Ann and I teamed up to work together exactly because of the reasons mentioned above. We both had successful businesses, but missed the motivation and encouragement that working with like minded people brings – so CareerTrain, and this book, came into being. We hope you enjoy it.

PART 1

THE BASIC ADVICE INTERVIEW

What makes an interview effective? If we can answer this, we are well on the way to being able to assess and improve our own practice. In 2004, researchers studied 50 guidance interviews. They asked clients, advisers and an expert witness to rate how effective the interviews were, and identified what actually takes place in guidance interviews evaluated as effective (Bimrose, Barnes, Hughes and Orton, 2004). They found that the best interviews incorporate four main activities (incorporating ten sub categories), paraphrased below:-

Building a working alliance
- Scene setting
- Rapport building

Exploring potential
- Gathering information
  a. Hard factual data
  b. Soft data - feelings, motivations, etc

Identifying options and strategies
- Giving information to clients
- Giving advice – making suggestions
- Giving guidance and using counselling skills to bring about change in thinking or behaviour

Ending and follow through
- Identifying goals
- Identifying action needed to achieve the goals
- Final summary, usually combined with writing an action plan
- Follow-through – referral, enabling, advocacy, follow-up

In an earlier piece of research, a member of the then Department of Employment's Careers Service Inspectorate studied a large number of careers interviews carried out in secondary schools. From this, he drew conclusions about what made the difference between a successful advice interview and a less effective one. He identified seven activities that the adviser needed to do (Bedford, 1982).

While the 2004 research looks at three levels of helping: (Information, Advice and Guidance), Bedford's interview model focuses more on providing information. His model is very similar to the later one in its early stages, but in focusing on providing information rather than in-depth guidance, it seems more relevant to people offering information and advice. For this reason, we offer you Bedford's model here, and explore the full guidance interview in the next section.

Bedford's seven activities are presented here in a list, and generally we would expect them to occur in this order. However, we would never insist on a rigid structure, so that you have the flexibility to decide when it is appropriate to introduce a topic. Also, there are a number of the activities that either should be happening throughout the interview or re-occurring at various stages in the interview.

Two of the seven activities were identified as key for an interview to be useful for the client:

 creating a friendly, encouraging atmosphere

and

 identifying client's needs accurately

Structuring Your Interview:
Bedford's 7 Essentials

 1. Create a friendly, encouraging atmosphere

 2. Establish the broad purpose of the interview

 3. Gather information from the client

 4. Identify the client's needs

 5. Give information to the client

 6. Summarise progress made during interview

 7. Clarify the next steps to be taken

1. Create a friendly, encouraging atmosphere

WHY?
What does this mean?

Would you like to be advised by someone who scared you? Or who disapproved of you? Would you open up and tell them your real hopes, fears, uncertainties?

Creating a friendly, encouraging atmosphere was one of the activities Bedford found to be a key factor if young people were to view their careers interviews as helpful.

The work of Carl Rogers reinforces this. He was a psychotherapist working in the USA in the mid 20th Century. He revolutionised attitudes with his philosophy of person-centred counselling, believing that the quality of the relationship between client and helper was more important than the skill and knowledge of the helper in enabling the client to make progress. He asks us not to hide behind the mask of professionalism, but to engage with the clients as ourselves, to build a natural, genuinely empathic relationship with them (Rogers, 1967).

In order to create this high quality relationship, he believed a helper should be able to feel and demonstrate three things if the client is to feel comfortable, relaxed and safe enough to benefit:

1. Empathic Understanding
2. Unconditional Positive Regard
3. Congruence

These are not easy concepts on first reading – we will explain!

1. **Understanding** or **Empathy**

Who would we choose to discuss our questions and worries with? Probably not someone who would say "Don't worry, you'll be OK". We'd prefer someone who shows they can see why we are worried - even if the same thing would not concern them. We want them to understand not just the facts, but also our feelings. We need them to show in some way that they have understood, not just by saying "I understand" but proving it by the way they respond.

Ways to show empathy include: reflecting back a summary, eg:

➢ You are afraid you'll lose your friends if you go away to college
➢ You feel a bit of a failure having to ask for advice?
➢ You are afraid of the treatment and you hate not knowing what to expect

It is not always necessary to explain why we think they are feeling afraid or angry or sad; in fact we should be very tentative about interpreting the client's feelings, if possible letting them expand in their own words, for example:

➢ It seems that upset you quite a lot....
➢ It's frustrating...
➢ The way you said that, you seem pretty angry

We don't even have to say anything: we can show empathy non-verbally with facial expressions and movements that aim to reflect what the other person is feeling, for example a gentle nod, a sympathetic frown, a sigh or a wry smile.

2. Acceptance and Liking or Unconditional Positive Regard

When we ask for help, we do not want to feel judged or disapproved of. We want the helper to feel positive towards us, even if we have made mistakes or done things we are not proud of. Key phrases are **non-judgemental**, **respect** and **prizing**. This acceptance needs to be **unconditional**, meaning that we can still value a person even if they have done or said things that we cannot agree with.

Of course this is very hard (impossible?) to do in all situations, but the aim is to see the *person* as separate from the *deeds*. If we have made mistakes in our own lives, we would want our helper to be non-judgemental, and see the person underneath. There will be times when a person has done certain things or is expressing certain view which make it impossible for us to feel positive towards them. In such cases we need to recognise this and consider referring them to another helper or agency, rather than try to continue working with them, since we are also aiming to show...

3. Being Genuine or Congruence

Have you ever felt that although someone said they liked you or agreed with you, you could not believe them?
  - Oh poor you, it must be awful for you
  - Yeah?
  - Amazing

I can tell whether you mean it when you respond to something I'm telling you, just as I can tell you've probably lost interest when your eyes wander to the other side of the room or you starting shifting around in your seat.

As an adviser, I may like to think that in situations where I cannot empathise with a client or feel positive towards them, I can be professional and act as though I do. But the client will know: our non verbal communication or body language will almost always reveal our true feelings. Research has shown that when there is conflict between our words ("It's good to see you...") and our body language (scowl, no eye contact), it is the body language that will be believed (see Part 3 - The Toolkit – First Impressions).

It is important to remember that words, voice and appearance need to send the same message - which is what being congruent means. If we do not do this, the recipient will either be confused or draw wrong conclusions. In order to demonstrate empathy and unconditional positive regard, we have to really feel them.

First Impressions Last

There is a generally accepted view, in the study of communication, that when people meet for the first time, their first impression (in the first few moments) has the most impact and colours their view of everything that happens afterwards. If we accept this to be true, it is clear that our feelings and attitudes towards the client are the first things we need to work on. This will include not only their perception of you, but also the organisation you work for and the quality of the service you provide.

 # LACK OF SELF AWARENESS

Here's a true story. A woman went to her local Jobcentre. She was a single parent, and as her youngest child had reached sixteen, she was required to make herself available for work. As you can imagine, she was very nervous, as she had never been to a Jobcentre before, and had not worked for many years. The Adviser was word perfect in taking her through the forms and procedures that needed to be completed. Half way through, the woman burst into tears and fled. The Adviser turned to a colleague: "What did I say?"

The Adviser had **said** nothing wrong – but she was completely oblivious to her tone and manner. She had fired questions as if they were coming from a machine gun, her tone of voice was harsh, her facial expression was as hard as rock, showing no understanding or compassion. The moral of the story is this: we need to be aware how our personal style – voice, body language, appearance, impacts on our clients. It is not easy to get an honest appraisal of the impact we make, but we need it if we are to reflect on our practice.

How to Create a Friendly, Encouraging Atmosphere

Publicity

You can begin to create the right environment even before the client meets you. The way you advertise your service in a leaflet, on a website, on a poster, can make clients expect to feel comfortable with you. You can use photographs and language, even accent, to make a diverse range of your whole potential client group feel they will be equally welcome. You can go to where clients are to advertise your service, rather than wait for them to find you. For clients likely to lack confidence, you can build a relationship first with those who already work with them (community workers, health visitors...). Sometimes, you can introduce yourself to clients in a group setting, so they can take a look at you in the safe anonymity of the group before meeting you face to face. Group introductions are often possible in school or college settings, or at the workplace during redundancy programmes.

Physical surroundings

Here are some things to consider. You may be in a position to influence the surroundings in which you meet clients. If you can't influence your surroundings, you can be aware of how they might affect the client and take extra trouble to make him feel at ease and welcome.

- Finding the way. Have clients been given clear instructions, can they park easily, are the bus stops close by, are you well signposted?

- Feeling at Home? Clients may lack confidence, and will be most comfortable in surroundings that feel familiar. This means different clients will feel most comfortable in different surroundings.

- Smart or Informal? All clients will probably feel most comfortable in surroundings that are clean, safe and healthy. However some may feel uncomfortable in a very smart, businesslike environment. If they are coming in with children, they may prefer it a bit lived in so that they won't be embarrassed if their children make a mess.

- Quiet or Bustling? Some clients will prefer quiet surroundings, others will be more comfortable if music is playing, or there is the sound of chatter and other people around. Some like being in a private area, others would feel threatened by this.

- Pictures and other images can make a client feel welcome and can stimulate their interests and inform them. However, be aware of any pictures and posters that could convey hostile messages to clients. Take a look at your surroundings with fresh eyes.

- Sit or stand? Some clients like to sit down (easy chairs or higher chairs round a table?) while others might feel this requires too much commitment from them, and they want to feel they can get away quickly after they have asked their question. Any interaction lasting more than a few minutes is likely to be more relaxed if you are both sitting down, preferably on the same type of chairs, certainly chairs that have you both at the same height. People often feel there should not be a desk between you and the client; if a desk or table will be needed, it is often more friendly to sit side by side or at right angles to the client. Sometimes clients may feel too exposed if there is not a table in front of them, and they will not want to sit too close to you. You need to be aware of different needs for personal space (and indeed eye contact) in different cultures.

- Physical disability. Clients with mobility difficulties, eg: wheelchair users or those on sticks or crutches, will feel most comfortable if they can enter easily, preferably without having to ask for help. Clients with painful backs or joints may be more comfortable sitting in higher chairs, perhaps with arms.

- Children. Some clients can't attend without their children. You may have access to a crèche, or you may provide a toy box to keep the children amused for a while.

- Privacy. Most people will not want others to overhear their questions and concerns. They may simply be embarrassed but they may also have sensitive issues to tell you about. How public is the area where you see clients? On the other hand, some clients may feel anxious or vulnerable if you take them off into a private room too soon.

Body Language

Before you even start speaking with a client, your body language will (or will not) be conveying empathy and unconditional positive regard. Some basic courtesies are:

- Look up immediately as the client approaches (stopping other conversation or activity), make eye contact and smile
- Open posture, facing client
- Relaxed, calm movements
- Non-verbal or minimal encouragers (nod, smile, "Right", "OK", "Mmm", "I see", "Yes?")

Never mind the body language, just fix the feelings!

Rather than worry too much about body language, if you feel interest and unconditional positive regard for the client, it will show (and the reverse will show too). This is why Carl Rogers says helpers need to be genuine (Rogers, 1967). Are you thinking:

> ➢ How nice to see you, I am going to enjoy answering your questions and working with you

or

> ➢ Oh no, not another one, I'm too busy

or

> ➢ I don't like the look of him, he's going to be trouble?

23

Whichever you are thinking, your body language will show it.

How to fix our Feelings

Remembering Rogers' three necessary conditions of Congruence, Unconditional Positive Regard and Empathic Understanding, we need to make sure our mindset is client-centred before we engage with a client. We may need to take a few moments to reflect, to think about how we feel, prepare to focus on them and their needs, even if they reveal aspects of themselves we find distasteful.

The Greeting

Different clients will feel comfortable with different approaches. You can decide which is more appropriate for each client:

- To shake hands *or* not to shake hands?
- "Good Morning" or "Hello" or "All right mate?" *or* "Hiya"?
- Polite and businesslike *or* gentle and warm *or* lively and fun?

A client-centred adviser will not say "I always shake hands" or "I always say Good Morning"; they will make judgements about whether each client they see is likely to be comfortable with a handshake, being offered tea/coffee, etc. They are flexible enough to adapt their welcome to each one.

It's OK to be yourself. Being genuine, you cannot be expected to turn into someone you clearly are not. You are simply remaining aware of how you can best create a friendly, encouraging atmosphere for each individual client.

General chat will give the client time to relax and get their bearings. You will decide which would be appropriate depending on the person and the situation, for example:-

- A question (about their journey, about the weather)
- A remark (the weather, the surroundings, noises)

- An apology (the delay, noises, the surroundings)
- A compliment (their baby, their hair, their bike, their efficiency)

But...be careful with compliments – they need to be appropriate and genuine – it is very easy for a compliment to sound false or patronising, or just too familiar and personal.

All this is designed to make the client feel comfortable, and remember that however they present themselves, they are likely to be lacking in confidence, in a new place, probably in a situation they are not happy with. See in Part 3 The Toolkit - Build them up Buttercup.

Throughout the interview

Although the friendly, encouraging atmosphere has to be created from the start, of course it needs to be maintained throughout the interview. The way you respond to what the client says needs to show that you respect them as an equal, that they have your full attention, that you want to understand them, and that you respect their right to decide whether or not to act upon your advice.

Sometimes it's Hard
to Create a Friendly, Encouraging Atmosphere

It can be hard...

- ..**to maintain the balance** between being friendly and getting the job done; between the person and the task; between the feelings and the facts. People tend to fall into one of two types: those whose natural tendency is to focus on people and feelings or those who tend to focus on the task and the facts. A focus on feelings is needed to help your clients feel comfortable and a focus on the task is needed for them to get what they came for. The model presented by the 2004 research into successful interviews (Bimrose et al., 2004) tells us we need to gather two types of information from the client: 1 - Hard factual data (achievements, skills, career history) and 2 - Soft data (feelings, motivations, preferences, awareness, interests).

As an adviser, each of us needs to recognise whether we are best at facts or feelings, and remember not to neglect the one that comes less naturally to us. Are YOU more comfortable talking about facts or about feelings? If you are not sure what this means, psychometric instruments such as Cattell's 16PF or Myers-Briggs Type Indicator, or other personality questionnaires such as those based on Holland's career types or Belbin's team roles are one way to explore your own preferences and personal style (see Part 3 The Toolkit – One Size Fits All?)

- **..to feel empathy and unconditional positive** regard for some people, especially if they are unpleasant to us, or if they annoy us in some way. Carl Rogers himself admitted it was hard! We need to be both honest and assertive: honest to recognise our own feelings and work at seeing things from the client's point of view; assertive to believe that in this equal relationship we are trying to build with the client, we also deserve respect and fair treatment.

We can establish boundaries with the client as to what is acceptable behaviour and the amount of effort they have to put into getting what they want. The next activity "Contracting" provides a time when you can start to establish boundaries. This should be done partly at the start of the meeting (or even beforehand in your publicity material) and then at any point when you feel the interaction is going in a direction that is not desirable.

Examples of re-visiting boundaries part way through an interaction are:

> You remember when we started working together, you agreed that the guidance would only work for you if we both work together, and treat each other with respect? By

26

missing appointments and not letting me know, I feel you are not treating me fairly.

➤ From the way you are sitting, not looking at me and not saying much, I get the feeling you are angry, and don't want to work with me. Am I right?

Read more about the technique of Immediacy in Part 3.

- **...to create a friendly, encouraging atmosphere when I'm under pressure**. Feeling rushed, or upset by something that has just happened, will make you tense and perhaps short-tempered, particularly if you were already feeling tired or unwell. Even though it will take an extra five minutes, you could try taking a breather between each client. Ideally you can get up, go for a breath of air or glass of water, and at the same time take a few deep breaths (count to five as you breathe in, five as you breathe out) ideally with your eyes closed, imagining a calm, relaxing scene (palm beach, scented flower garden). As you do so, tell yourself that you are feeling calm, that you will be able to focus on the client as a person worthy of care and respect, seeing the world through their eyes, and that you want to create a friendly, encouraging atmosphere for them.

2. Establish the purpose of the interview

Also known as CONTRACTING

When a client makes contact with an information, advice and guidance service, they will have a purpose in mind and hope to gain something from this interaction.

When responding to the enquiry, you as the adviser will respond to what you believe the client wants.

Why should you contract? If you don't, what could go wrong?

Debbie came to the advice centre asking about computer training.

The adviser thought she wanted to enrol on one of the courses offered by the centre. He brought out the list of courses offered and talked Debbie through each of them, explaining the pro's and con's of each.

Debbie appeared to be losing interest and ended by saying she'd take the list and think about it before deciding.

When she was telephoned to follow up on the session, she said she had now decided to go into child care work instead. She had not found the advice session useful because she had not really wanted to go into computer work, she just wanted to find out whether it would suit her and also find out about other career options.

Maggie phoned the advice line to ask about child care. She was having to leave her children alone while she went to work. After listening sympathetically, the adviser told Maggie she may have to pass on to others the fact that the children were being left. If Maggie had known this, she would not have revealed so much to the adviser. She immediately put the phone down. She felt anxious, but also angry and alienated, that everyone was against her and she would never be able to move forward and create a better life for her family.

John called into the advice centre during his lunch break. After a short wait, the adviser saw him, was very helpful and offered information on the topics that interested him. He needed to print a copy off. He was gone some time and when he returned, John was very agitated. He had not realised how long it would take, and now his parking ticket had run out and he would be late back to work.

It is professional good practice to ensure that a contract is negotiated at the start of any information, advice or guidance interaction, because it is important that both client and adviser have the same purpose, or expect the same outcome. If this is not clearly stated and agreed, preferably near the start of the interaction...

...you risk wasting:-   ... the client may be:-   ...and lose:-

- Time
- Effort

- Disappointed
- Frustrated
- Confused

- Confidence
- Motivation

What should you contract about?

The contract should cover:-

1. The Process or Mechanics of the interview
2. The Content or Scope of your service
3. The Ethical Boundaries

1 Process	2 Content or Scope	3 Ethical Boundaries
Timing • How long will the interaction take? • How many times can the client return for further advice? • When and how can they make follow up appointments? • Where will it take place? **Cost** • Is advice free? • If not, how much? • Is there any subsidy? **Written records** • If you take notes, what are they used for? • Will the client receive any written information?	**Roles & Responsibilities** • What can you help with? • What can you not help with? • Can you refer on to others within or outside your organisation? If so, what can they offer? • What is the client expected to do? **Structure** • What will be discussed during the interaction, and in what order? • How will you work with the client (eg: in groups, one-to-one, is the client expected to listen, to speak, to produce written work)?	**Impartiality** • Is your information comprehensive, or is it limited to one provider or one type of provider? • Is your advice completely client-centred and independent, or do you have loyalty to an organisation or a policy? **Confidentiality** • Who else, apart from you and the client, will be told about what is discussed? • How is the client's personal information protected from being seen by others? • When will any records be destroyed?

How can you contract with the client?

If you go through the whole of the list above, you will have made a speech that bores the client rigid, and takes up most of the time allocated for the session. So how should you balance the need to contract and ensure clarity with the need to maintain your friendly, encouraging atmosphere and keep the client interested? As always in advice interviews, the aim is to empower and respect the client, partly by letting them have as much input as possible. Try this:

First check what the client expects from you, and then confirm or correct this. This can be done with open questions like:

- ➢ What can we do for you?
- ➢ How can I help you?
- ➢ What are you looking for?
- ➢ What's brought you here today?
- ➢ How much time have you got?
- ➢ What do you know about us?

Once the client has answered, you can fill the gaps in his/her understanding of your service, eg:

> I can give you information on the courses, **but** for guidance on whether they are right for you, I can make you an appointment with the careers adviser.

> I can spend up to 15 minutes with you now. If you need more time, you can make as many appointments as you like for future dates.

Sometimes it's hard
to contract effectively

It's hard to...

...remember to contract. We will be keen to respond to the client's requests, to show that we can help, and to get on with the job in the limited time available. It may be only later that we realise the client had different expectations and is now disappointed and feels he has wasted his time with us.

...keep it short and simple. The list of things that the client needs to understand about the way you are able to work with them is so long that you could spend the whole interview listing them while the client sits there wondering when you are going to start answering their questions. A long speech can destroy the work you have been doing to build a friendly, encouraging atmosphere.

Try these solutions:-

Giving out a leaflet before the interview stating many of the conditions ("What you can expect from the advice session") and when they arrive, on introducing yourself simply asking if they have read it and if they have any questions about it.

Asking the client what she wants to get out of the session, probing further to make clear her expectations. Responding to each point as she makes it will turn the contracting into a natural conversation rather than a long speech from you. You may even ask the client to write down in advance what she wants from the session.

Re-contracting: You can return to the contract and if necessary re-contract throughout the interview if you feel it is straying from the point. Re-contracting is also useful if the client appears not to have fully understood what you can and can't offer, or if you can no longer deliver what you had promised (for example, it is taking longer than you thought to deal with the issues raised). See Part 3 The Toolkit - Challenging – Steering for more about re-contracting to help keep the focus and structure of the interview.

OVER THE BOUNDARY

Possibly the most potentially dangerous of all the dangers is the issue of boundaries. In any role where your purpose is to build a helping relationship with another person, it is sometimes difficult to know where to stop. We are asked to be client-centred, to put their needs at the centre of all we do. But does this mean we have to give the client everything they ask for, or everything we can see they need? Of course not, or we could end up working 24 hours every day, taking clients home with us, sharing with them all we have.

So where do you set the boundaries between what you will and won't do to help a client? It is very important to know what your limits are in advance, because you may find you could be persuaded to overstep them for a client who is particularly vulnerable or desperate, or especially good at appealing to your parenting instinct, or any feelings of guilt you may have. Relationship building can lead us into the temptation of blurring other boundaries. In a normal relationship, people interact as equals. Each person may confide in the other, tell them their worries, be playful together. They may become friends, even lovers. In our role (whether paid or voluntary) as adviser, we and the client are not friends interacting on an equal basis. The adviser is the professional, we have a duty of care, to ensure that while we encourage clients to be open and honest with us, we treat them with respect and we do not abuse that privilege. This is why most professions have their own Code of Ethics or Principles. Professional bodies of relevance to people working in Information, Advice and Guidance for Learning and Work are ICG (Institute of Career Guidance) and NAEGA (National Association for Educational Guidance for Adults). See Bibliography section for their contact details to find out about their codes.

Although we can't imagine we would cross these ethical boundaries, unfortunately there have been stories in the press of people who have. It is not so difficult to imagine that when we are trying to build a friendly relationship, we could become emotionally involved with some clients who appeal to us in some way. All of us in advice and guidance enjoy helping people – that is why we chose this job rather than other (probably more lucrative) alternatives. The "damsel in distress" or the "neglected child" could strike a chord that attracts us inappropriately, perhaps especially at times when our own relationships are not at their best.

If you feel the slightest inkling that this may be happening to you, please, please seek help. Ideally your organisation will have some kind of supervision arrangement for support. If you cannot take this worry to a manager, colleague, or mentor, look for a BACP registered counsellor (www.bacp.co.uk) and talk it through in total confidence.

On the other side of the coin, even though we have no such feelings, some clients may misinterpret our concern as something else, and may develop an attraction to us. Again, if you have any suspicion this is happening, share this with someone at the earliest stage and get advice on how to cover yourself against complaints or compromising situations. Until the boundaries are clear and you feel safe, you may be wise to avoid further contact with the client.

Finally, we need to be fully aware of the limitations of our own competence. It is relatively easy to be aware of the boundaries of our factual knowledge. I know a lot about careers in the social and care sector, but my understanding of science and engineering is limited. It is sometimes harder to recognise the limits of our skills and competence. It is important to recognise whether we are equipped to help the client over the boundary between advice and guidance. It is also essential to recognise when a client needs more therapeutic help, to deal with an issue that is outside our competence, for example relationship or bereavement counselling. Ideally we will know of people or agencies that are qualified in these areas, so that we can offer to refer clients to them for the help they need.

3. Gather information from the client

What do you need to know?

Now that the client feels welcome and relaxed, and you have contracted to set the boundaries of the interaction, you are ready to start the real business of the interview.

What do you want me to do for you? What do you need?

The first thing you need to find out is what they want from you and your service. A client will probably come to you with a presenting question. Let's take two examples and then explore what information you need to gather from the client before you can provide a sensible answer.

Example 1
Presenting question to a careers or educational adviser:

➤ How can I become a qualified carpenter?

You could just hand the client a long information sheet giving all the answers. Even then, however, this sheet may not have all the information about local opportunities. So in order to give an appropriate answer, you need some information about the client. For example, you probably need to know:

➤ How old are you?
  (still young enough to qualify for an apprenticeship?)
➤ What qualifications have you got?
  (sufficient literacy and numeracy? Any previous training?)
➤ How much income do you need?
  (able to train full time on a low allowance?)
➤ What work are you doing now?
  (if already working for a builder, this would help)

You may also need to make sure you understand what the client means by the presenting question.

> What are your long-term career aims?
> Do you know what carpentry involves?
> How much thought have you given to whether this is the best career goal for you?
> Or is it just as a hobby?

Example 2
Presenting question to a Debt Counsellor:

> How can I clear my debts?

Information you need will probably include:

> How much do you owe?
> How much income do you have?
> What are your regular expenses?
> What could you give up?
> Who do you owe?
> ...and so on

How can you gather the information?

You could use a form to gather some basic factual details, but the usual way to gather information is by listening and questioning. This requires more skills than many people imagine. They are counselling skills, which can be learned and perfected via courses, by reading, by observing a skilled practitioner and by practice.

Active Listening

This means putting aside distractions and giving the client your full attention. Usually when we are listening, we are also doing other things – for example, if the radio is on when we are driving, the TV while we are cooking.... Even when we are having a conversation, often we are planning what we are going to say next while the other person is talking. This is fine for everyday living, but is not listening of sufficient quality for an advice session.

Active listening is very hard work, but it will result in you gaining a much greater insight into clients' needs: their circumstances, issues, feelings and priorities. We also need to show that we are listening, which can be done both physically through our body language and verbally in a range of ways from what are known as minimal encouragers (Mmmm, Ah, Oh, etc) to reflecting back what we are hearing through appropriate repetition or paraphrasing. Examples are given below in the paragraph headed "Helping the Client Tell their Story".

Non-verbal clues – being observant

Active listening involves being observant, watching as well as listening. You may pick up clues about what is really concerning a client, from an awareness of:

- Body: posture, movements, gestures of hands, feet, head, sudden stiffening or recoiling
- Facial expressions: smile, frown, tight lips, raised eyebrows, eyes staring or looking down, avoiding eye contact, suddenly stopping smiling
- Voice tone: loud, soft, strong, trembling, hesitating, emphasis, silence
- Physiological responses: blushing, paleness, perspiring, trembling, tearful

The client's non-verbal communication can:

- Strengthen or emphasise what they are saying, giving you a clue as to how important it is
- Alert you to any inconsistencies, where the client says something (e.g. they enjoy something) when their body, face and voice tone imply the opposite

This is not to suggest that we disbelieve the things our clients tell us, but rather that we look for evidence to corroborate their words. We can do this mostly by questioning and exploring to make sure we understand them, but also we can look at how they are presenting themselves. Are their words in harmony with their body language? Is the tone of voice what you would expect, given the issues? Often our true feelings are given away by how we speak or by our body language. (See First Impressions in Part 3). If there seems to be a mismatch, or mixed messages, there is some investigation to be done before we can find a way forward.

Non-verbal communication is helpful in giving clues, but it is important to check these out before drawing any conclusions. Think of body language as providing cues for your questions, eg:

- ➢ You say you want to train to be a teacher, but you don't seem very enthusiastic about the idea...
- ➢ I get the impression that you are a bit nervous about going to the evening class – am I right?

 ASSUMPTIONS

- A well spoken client with an executive job and wearing a college scarf has been through Higher Education.
- An illiterate client wants to learn to read and write.
- A parent wants to be able to support his children.
- A public school education will result in some qualifications.

These are all assumptions that we have made with particular clients – wrong every time. We do need to work from assumption sometimes, it can be a short cut – but be very wary. The key here is recognising the difference between assumption and fact (see Part 3: Offa's agenda). Be aware of assumptions you are making, and check them out.

Helping the Client Tell Their Story

Clients sometimes need help in telling their story, so there are things we can do and say to encourage and prompt them.

Prompting - Non verbal prompts and encouragement

We started to look at body language in the section on how to create a friendly, encouraging atmosphere. To show we are listening actively to a client, we can:

- Have our upper body (at least our head and shoulders) facing them
- Sit fairly still, making sure we are patient and relaxed, not tapping our feet or fingers
- Smile and nod to show interest in and approval of what the client is saying
- Maintain an open posture, no crossed arms or legs
- Lean slightly towards them, to show interest
- Look at them, making frequent eye contact (though not a fixed stare)
- Allow silence (don't immediately rush to fill the silence; if you relax and look interested the client may go on to give more detail)
- Try to mirror their posture or expressions (**if** we can do it naturally, in no way appearing to mimic — see more on mirroring in Part 3).

It is important to remember differing cultural norms and expectations in relation to body language. Our society is diverse and people from many different backgrounds will seek advice from us. What may appear to be friendly in one culture may be seen as disrespectful or invasion of privacy in another. This could involve levels of eye contact, how close we sit or approach, forms of address, what we wear or expect others to wear.

Conversely, we as advisers can also be shocked by our clients, and would need to decide whether to adjust our thinking so as to remain client-centred or to ask them to adjust their behaviour as a way of negotiating boundaries. If we are finding it difficult to know what is acceptable to the clients we meet, we should make a point of finding out: add this to your list of development needs (a form is provided at the back of this book) and perhaps discuss it in supervision or other support meetings. It is an important ethical and equality issue.

Prompting - Short verbal prompts or minimal encouragers

(especially important when interacting by telephone)

> Yes...
> I see...
> Oh...
> Mmm...
> Really?
> And then...?
> So...?
> Go on...
> Right...
> OK...

Questioning – Open Questions

Usually, open questions are more helpful than closed questions in encouraging people to express themselves. These are questions that cannot be answered by "Yes" or "No". For example:

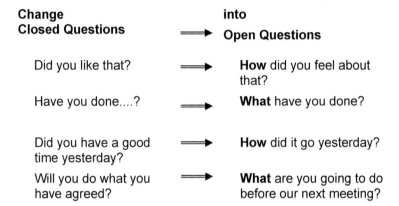

Change Closed Questions	into Open Questions
Did you like that?	**How** did you feel about that?
Have you done....?	**What** have you done?
Did you have a good time yesterday?	**How** did it go yesterday?
Will you do what you have agreed?	**What** are you going to do before our next meeting?

Open questions usually begin with:

> ➢ **What ....?**
> ➢ **How ....?**
> ➢ **Where....?**
> ➢ **When....?**
> ➢ **Who....?**
> ➢ **Why....?**

Our favourites (the most effective and least threatening) are:

> ➢ **What.... ?**
> ➢ **How.... ?**

We don't often like:

> ➢ **Why....?** (it's too broad - hard to answer - and it can sound critical or accusing)

43

Similar to open questions are requests for more detail such as:

- Tell me more about ....
- Can you describe ......

Closed Questions

There are times when you need to ask a closed question. For example, to clarify a specific piece of information:

- So did you attend the job interview at Smith's?
- Did you pass the English exam?

Questions as statements

Sometimes it can seem as though you are firing too many questions at the client, like an interrogation. You can vary the style by using statements such as:

- I'd like to know more about that
- I'm interested in what you said about that experience
- I'm wondering how you feel about that
- You say it didn't work out
- I'd like to hear what happened
- That sounds interesting

Overall, **gathering information** means **helping the client tell their story.** We should aim to:

- Allow silence (while looking interested and encouraging)
- Keep the pace slow and relaxed
- Ask only one question at a time
- Allow the client to answer the question (rather than answer it for them)
- Avoid interrupting the client but allow them to interrupt us
- Let the client come up with their own ideas first, before suggesting options
- Wait until we have gathered all the information we need before starting to provide answers
- Question sensitively and sparingly – it's not an interrogation
- Keep an open mind – don't try to interpret or explain at this stage
- Be transparent: explain to the client why we are asking the questions
- Make sure the client knows what will and won't be kept confidential

Above all, it is very important, in order to gather all the information you need in order to really help the client, that at this stage of the interview ...

... the client does most of the talking

- **More than 50% in the whole interview**
- **At least 75% at this information gathering stage.**

Try taping an interview, then listen to it with a stop watch to see who talks the most. If you are talking more than 25% in this information gathering stage, you have a development need! Add it to your Personal Development Plan and seek opportunities to improve your counselling skills.

Sometimes it's hard
to gather enough information

It's hard to....

...keep quiet. We feel that it's our job to provide the client with all the information they need, we are afraid they will go away empty handed, and that we are here to work. But in order to find out what information the client really needs, we need to give them the time and space to express themselves. We need to remember that they are on unfamiliar ground. They need time to understand the questions we are asking them and to work out the reply.

...listen attentively. When we listen to clients, what we hear can be distorted if we allow ourselves to...

- Be distracted (by our own thoughts, worries, time pressures, noises, the queue waiting)
- Judge or form an opinion on what the client is saying
- Listen only to facts while ignoring feelings
- Rehearse or plan our answer (to keep the conversation going or move on) rather than listen fully
- Feel sympathy, so that we are affected by the client's feelings (sympathy is not empathy)
- Interrupt (except when the client has lost their way in the story, and needs guiding)

It's hard to….

…ask the right questions. The **wrong** kinds of questions are usually:

- Closed Questions
  - ➢ Did you like Maths at school?
- Multiple Questions
  - ➢ How did you get on with Maths? Did you like it? What marks did you get? Did you like the teacher?
- Questions that are too wide open
  - ➢ What's the best thing you've ever done?
- Questions the client does not know the facts to answer
  - ➢ What kind of learning suits you best?
- "Why?" questions if they imply criticism and suggest the client must justify themselves
  - ➢ Why did you drop out of college?
- or if they are too broad, with many possible answers
  - ➢ Why are you unhappy?
- Leading Questions
  - ➢ Were you angry when she spoke to you like that?
- Questions that you then answer yourself
  - ➢ What hours could you work? I don't suppose you'd want full time with the children.
  - ➢ Could you sell one of your cars? I guess your partner wouldn't like that.

…get some clients to speak. Some will be more reserved than others. Asking the right kind of questions should help, while asking the wrong kind of questions will certainly discourage quieter clients from speaking. If they are reserved, we need to work harder at keeping quiet, we need to leave longer silences for them to think about their reply. However, at the start of the session, we may actually need to say a bit more about ourselves and our role, or talk about everyday matters – the weather, etc – in order to break the ice and give the client longer to relax and get their bearings before we put them in the spotlight. We can also find other ways of helping clients express themselves, perhaps through questionnaires, computer software or practical exercises such as card sorts (youth workers use an exercise The Rickter Scale® - see Bibliography). See Part 3 The Toolkit - Build them up, Buttercup and The Rickter Scale® for more ideas on how to help clients open up and engage with you.

...stop some clients from speaking. Some clients have so much on their minds that it all comes tumbling out and we feel overwhelmed and confused, unsure what their question is or where to start helping them. The skill of summarising can come in useful here –

> ➤ So let's stop a minute and see what you've said so far

– followed by a bullet point summary of the issues as you have understood them. If it is really impossible to stop the flow, you may need to add some body language to emphasise your attempt to structure the conversation. You could try: a decisive movement of the head; intake of breath to suggest you are going to speak; breaking eye contact; picking up a pen. It is important not to embarrass the client, who may be surprising themselves in how much they are saying now that they have found someone who will listen.

 FACE VALUE

Constraints on our time often pressurise us into dealing with clients as swiftly as we can. We may not be resourced to conduct a thorough exploration of the clients' issues. There is a big 'But', though. If we take their words at face value, we may do them, and ourselves, a disservice. What is the point of working towards building an action plan if the foundations aren't real?

4. Identify the client's needs

What does this mean?

Before you can help the client, you need to be sure you have found out what help they need.

Identifying the client's needs comes in three stages:

> **1. Analyse**
> **2. Summarise**
> **3. Check with the client – Did I get it right?**

1. Analyse

You need to make sense of all the information you have been gathering and sort it in your mind. You may be asking yourself if the client needs:

- Information – pure facts
- Advice - applying the facts to their own situation and deciding what to do next
- Guidance – more time to explore what they really want before deciding
- Assessing – finding out their current skill level, their preferred career type
- Enabling – help moving to the next stage, whether writing a CV, completing application forms, preparing for interviews, working out their finances, making contact with the right agencies
- Advocacy – help overcoming barriers and making their case to other agencies or people, possibly legal action
- Mentoring, coaching or other ongoing support – to help them develop new habits, to change their lifestyle
- Teaching – to help them learn new skills
- Counselling – to help them understand and overcome deeper confusion (cf NAEGA, 2003)

2. Summarise

Having worked out what they need, even if it is simply information, the next step is to summarise this, both for ourselves, so that we are clear what help and information we are going to give them, and for them, to check that we have understood correctly.

Summarising is an excellent way to stop ourselves rushing to answer the first issue raised by the client before making sure we have heard the whole story. If we summarise, it gives the client the chance to say:

➤ Yes that's right *or*

➤ No, you've misunderstood *or*

➤ Yes, but there's more... .

Summaries will often start with phrases like:-

➤ Before I give you the information, let me check I've understood....

➤ Are you saying that....

➤ So what you want to know is....

➤ So to summarise, you want...

➤ **As I understand it,** come 30th June you will be unemployed and homeless, so you need a job and somewhere to live. These issues are not too urgent because you can stay with your sister for a few weeks, and you have already made an appointment to register for Job Seekers Allowance. But you would much rather have a job and flat ready to move into, **so you want** to find out what sort of jobs you could apply for.

3. Check

Following your summary, you then ask the client:
> ➤ Have I got this right?

and allow him to correct you if necessary.

If the client says you have not got it right, you need to do some more listening, to let them correct you.

Summarise

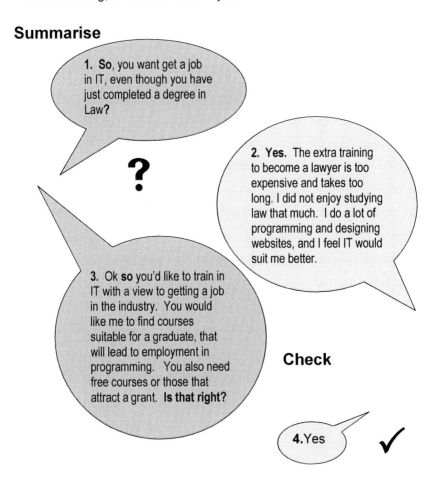

1. So, you want get a job in IT, even though you have just completed a degree in Law?

2. Yes. The extra training to become a lawyer is too expensive and takes too long. I did not enjoy studying law that much. I do a lot of programming and designing websites, and I feel IT would suit me better.

3. Ok **so** you'd like to train in IT with a view to getting a job in the industry. You would like me to find courses suitable for a graduate, that will lead to employment in programming. You also need free courses or those that attract a grant. **Is that right?**

Check

4. Yes

Sometimes it's Hard
to analyse, summarise and check

Summarising what the client has said before we go on to provide answers is surprisingly hard to do, perhaps because of these factors:

- **Pressure** We feel a pressure to get on with the job and provide answers promptly; perhaps we need to show outcomes
- **Wanting to help** We have built up a lot of useful knowledge and we want to use it to help the client
- **It's mentally demanding** Listening with the concentration required to analyse and organise the summary requires considerable mental effort: multi-tasking to perform on several levels at the same time, remembering to maintain the friendly, encouraging atmosphere and to enable the client to express themselves fully.

Summarising is a skill to work on but it will pay dividends, because:

- **It values the client** – it shows we have been listening and have understood their needs
- **It is efficient** – it prevents us wasting time giving out information the client does not need
- **It clarifies** the issues for the client – people do not always see their issues clearly, but once these have been clarified clients can sometimes work out the solutions for themselves
- **It empowers the client** both by enabling him to see and resolve his own issues and also by checking our summary with him, enabling him to correct any mistakes in our interpretation
- **It provides structure** to the interview. It rounds off the information gathering stage and sets the agenda for the next stage: providing information.

Interim summaries

Summarising can also be used throughout the information gathering stage to check each issue the client is raising and put it on your mental list to address later. This could include some re-contracting:

> ➤ Adviser: It seems that one of your difficulties is where you are living?
> ➤ Client: Yes
> ➤ Adviser: Although I can't help with that, there is a housing adviser you might like to meet and I can give you details before you go.

5. Give information to the client

What is information-giving?

AT LAST! Your chance to deliver! To give the client what they came for. To pass on the knowledge that will help them.

Now that you have listened attentively and made sure you fully understand what the client wants and needs, you should be in a position to provide them with high quality information.

High quality information is....

- Accurate
- Comprehensive
- Up to date
- Impartial

But it is also....

- Relevant to the individual's needs
- Interesting
- Digestible
- Understandable
- Useable

LANGUAGE, TIMOTHY!

Beware of jargon, acronyms, slang, regional idiosyncrasies, eduspeak, psychobabble, and all other languages that may confuse your client. We can also irritate our client by being patronising, using big and clever words, clichés, and phrases fresh from government policy or management training. Choose your words to match your client's needs, not your own.

(if you are under 40, you may not remember that 'Language, Timothy!' was a catchphrase from the sitcom "Sorry!". Ronnie Corbett played the down trodden Timothy, whose mother constantly told him off)

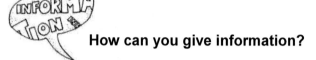 **How can you give information?**

Information does not only have to be provided by the spoken word. It can also be offered:

- In writing - written by you to suit this client, on paper or email
- Printed materials - leaflets, information sheets, etc
- Audio-Visually - a video perhaps, or a CD
- By Computer (plus perhaps a printout) - from software on site or via websites

How you give information will vary according to the client

- **A client unable to read fluently** would prefer very little written information, just essentials such as addresses and names, plus basic leaflets, and perhaps the suggestion that they show it to a friend or relative. You may need to make more use of the spoken word and/or visual material.

- **We can confuse with too many words** if we are not careful. As advisers, most of us enjoy speaking and listening, and words are our trade. Many people do not use language so much in their daily lives - this does not mean they are not able, but their skills lie elsewhere, for example in practical work, number, computing, science, design. Some people can understand things better if presented in visual form such as diagrams.

- **A well-qualified client who is short of time** may prefer written information to take away and study at leisure rather than a lot of spoken detail.

- **A client whose first language is not English** may (or may not – you need to check) find it easier to read English than to listen to it.

- **A client wanting to choose between a wide range of options** may need the information broken down into manageable chunks, perhaps returning for more detailed information when they have made some basic choices and narrowed down options.

- **A client who is familiar with the subject** being discussed can take in more than someone to whom everything about it is new.

- **Technical terms, jargon and initials.** We must make sure the terms we use are understood by the general public and by this particular client. "Distance learning package", "NVQ", "key skills" are some terms very familiar to us, but we need to check clients' understanding of these.

- **Intellectual ability** - some people have the capacity to grasp new information and concepts more quickly than others. Everyone needs information presented to them in bite sized chunks - you need to find out what is bite-sized for each individual client.

- **Physical ability** - hearing impairment is an obvious barrier to understanding information presented orally, visual impairment to information presented in writing. How can we overcome these barriers? Have we suitable materials, equipment or technology (or people)?

Finally
Check the client has understood

It is not usually enough to ask: "Do you understand?" and accept "Yes" from the client. Many clients will not dare to say "No", or they may be still trying to take in all the information and unsure yet whether they have fully understood it. Instead, try:

➤ Have you any further questions?

or better still, open questions such as:

➤ What do you think?
➤ How do you feel about what I've told you?
➤ So what are you going to do now?"

 # INFORMATION DUMPING

If there was an award for The Most Committed Sin in guidance practice, this would be it. Ok, there are times, and even jobs, where we are required just to inform clients, but we need to find out what the client already knows before we spout forth, so that we can build on their understanding and select relevant input. Often our intentions are good - the client says they want an IT course / to be a mechanic / a new CV. This is something we know about, so filled with enthusiasm and a desire to help (or be seen as helpful and knowledgeable) we gleefully tell the client all we know, maybe burying them in leaflets along the way. Job done. Information dumped.

An IT helpdesk technician took a call asking how to change the background on a picture. Imagine you were that caller. The technician launched into a detailed explanation of the system capacity, why the best software wasn't available, other options, all in unintelligible technobabble. How would you have felt? Do you know how to fix your picture yet?

Read more about this in Part 3, see especially How we Learn.

6. Summarise progress made during interview

Summarising (again, at the end of the interview) will help you check that you have given the client what they came for, and help them to understand the information given.

It is a summary of what the client wanted to know, what has been discussed, and what information you have given the client. This can be done orally or on paper (some advice and guidance organisations provide a written summary of guidance).

HOW
can you Summarise?

You have already summarised your understanding of the client's needs before you started to give information. Now that you have given the information you will put the whole thing into context for the client by going back to the start to sum up the whole session (or even the whole interaction which may have started at an earlier session). You may start something like this:

> Let's look at what we have discussed...

> ...You asked for information on computer courses...

> ...We found that you may also need to brush up on your written English...

> ...I told you about 2 different basic skills programmes, one here at the centre and also an evening class at XX College...

- ...I also told you about the "IT for the Terrified" course we run at the centre...
- ...You decided to sign up for both courses at the centre, to start next week...
- ...You have also taken information on careers in office work, to read for the future.

And after your summary DON'T FORGET...

ASK the client.... to **check** "Is that right? Do you agree?"

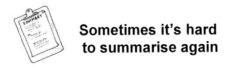

Sometimes it's hard to summarise again

I haven't got time

Time pressures will always be an issue, but if the client understands the reasons behind the advice, he is so much more likely to act upon it. We can never under-estimate how much new information a client has had to take in during an advice session. The information we give clients is so very familiar to us, because we work with it every day. We know why we have made the suggestions, we truly believe they are best for the client. But it is a real waste if the client goes away without a clear idea of not only what he is to do, but why: how it fits in with his overall goal, and how it will meet his needs. Read more about this in Part 3 How We Learn.

Let the client summarise

Rather than summarising for the client, or writing a summary for the client then reading it to them, ask them...

Waiting for them to reply will be more time-consuming than summarising for them, but will pay dividends by reassuring you that they have understood what has been going on and that they are committed to any decisions made. It is empowering, enabling and client-centred advice.

A written summary

Many advisers have a pad of carbonated forms to give clients at the end of a session. To help you write a summary before stating the action that has been agreed (see next section) the form is split into two main parts:

1. Summary – What was discussed
2. Action agreed

This should be compiled **jointly with the client** at the end of the session

7. Clarify the next steps : the Action Plan

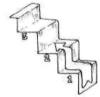

WHY?

As your aim is to help the client move forward, you will want to ensure that she knows what to do next, to move towards her goal. Now you have reached the final stage of the interview, you will ensure that the client is ready to take the first, practical steps.

WHAT and HOW?

This will usually be a list of things to do, perhaps set out in order, ideally with dates by which time each action should be taken.

It is often written down (although it does not have to be, it can be done orally) in the form of an action plan.

You can find suggestions as to what an action plan should include in various documents.

Gerard Egan (1994) gives us:

"Three simple questions.
1. What concrete things need to be done ....?
2. In what sequence should these be done?....
3. What is the time frame?"

Rosemary Jolley (2001) suggests a plan should state clearly the objective to be achieved with "a number of different suggested routes or options to achieve that end". It should:

"Include six key elements:
- Priorities of action with appropriate timescales
- Who the guidance worker and client need to see and who to contact
- Supporting information to aid access (for example, time of appointment, how to get to a college and location of tutor's office)
- Key questions for guidance worker and client to remember to ask
- What action to be taken by each as a result
- What follow-up has been arranged by the guidance worker to check on the progress of the client through the plan"

If you are working to a contract under a particular funding initiative, you will probably find there are specific requirements, probably including the above, but maybe with additional information that you must incorporate into the action plan.

Signposting and Referral

As has been suggested above, the client's next steps will often including approaching another organisation for help putting their plan into effect. In advice and guidance for learning and work, it will often be a learning provider: a college or course tutor. It may be an agency that can provide support you are unable to offer: in the section on identifying the client's needs, we saw that needs often become apparent that you are not equipped to meet (housing, drug or alcohol dependency, child care, support for ex-offenders, or for people with disabilities).

Signposting tends to mean giving the client the agency's details so that they can make contact as and when they wish. Referring means that we take some action to enable that referral, perhaps making a phone call to arrange an appointment for them, perhaps completing agreed referral forms.

When we signpost or refer a client, we need to explain clearly why we think that agency is suitable, respecting the client's right to accept or reject this referral. In referring, we need to agree in advance with the client which of their personal details can be passed on.

It's the client's action plan

In clarifying next steps, it is important (as always) to involve the client. You can ask them to tell you what they are going to do, and then perhaps write it down as they speak, or maybe let them write it down. The best way to empower clients to take charge of their own lives is to do as little as possible for them, only intervening when they need more information or get stuck. At the very least, you will ask them to sign their agreement to a written action plan, and confirm that the action planned is action they wish and intend to take.

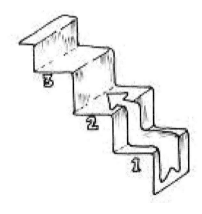

Sometimes it's hard to be sure the client will take the action agreed

Will the client take the action?

Sometimes we can tell that the client is just going through the motions and is not going to take the action planned. Or, we may be shocked and disappointed to discover later that they did not. Perhaps this is because they were not involved in planning the action, and did not really want to commit to it. Involving the client every step of the way, asking them what ideas they have, what they are going to do rather than advising them what to do, will ensure that the plan is their plan, not ours.

 OWNERSHIP

A young mum went to an enthusiastic new Adviser and said she thought she'd like to be a hairdresser. SuperAdviser sprang into action, pulled strings, secured a college place, sourced funding for the kit, found a childcare place, even the nursery costs. The client was informed of all of this – and didn't turn up to college. She had wanted to mull over the idea and find out what it may involve, she was nowhere near ready to leap into it. The chastened Adviser learnt a swift lesson in the importance of exploring what the client feels, knows, and understands, and letting them take ownership of the decision making process.

It takes time to involve the client

We have already acknowledged that most of us are pressed for time. We can see the queue of clients waiting, or we have a million other tasks awaiting us. It is so easy to write the prescription and hand it to the client, possibly only asking them for a signature because we need it for our statistics or as quality assurance for our funding contract. We need to remind ourselves that time taken now to involve the client should save time later, avoiding the need to revisit the issue because it was not clearly agreed the first time.

SMART plans

Sometimes action plans are so vague that it is hard to get started on them or to know when they have been achieved. "You will apply for a degree course in Medicine". "I will lose weight". SMART is an acronym to tighten up that plan.

- **Specific** - How specific is the plan? Is it clear exactly what needs to be done?
- **Measurable** – Will you and the client be able to tell when they have taken the action?
- **Appealing** – Does that client really want to take this action or are they afraid or bored by the idea?
- **Realistic** – How easy will it be for the client to take the steps planned? Have they got the abilities, the support, is it achievable?
- **Time bound** – Have you set deadline dates for each specific action?

See Part 3 for more examples of SMART goals.

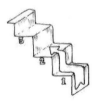

On the next page is an example of an Action Plan, using a set form:

Summary of Guidance and Action Plan for__Gary Smith____

Where you are now

Working in a warehouse, loading and unloading lorries. Want a better job. Age 17,
No qualifications from school. Quite good at figure work but find reading and
writing difficult. Not sure what level you are at.

Where you want to be / Your goal(s)

Skilled and qualified car body repairer/panel beater. (by age 21)

Job ad's need level 2 in Vehicle Body and Paint operations.

Get these qualifications by doing an Apprenticeship or college course.

They often need GCSE grade D in Maths and English or a Foundation Diploma, or
other Level 1 qualification.

Medium term goals are:

1st choice – get a job as an Apprentice or

2nd choice – get on a Motor Vehicle course at college

Short term goals:

See if you can get an apprenticeship now

Get an assessment of your Maths and English

Get English and Maths to the level wanted by colleges and employers

How you are going to get there / Your Action Plan

Action	Target Date
Go to Connexions and ask for names of employers offering Apprenticeships in Body Repair.	30 Jan
Either you or Connexions to phone these employers to apply for the jobs.	7 Feb
If no luck, get an assessment of your English and Maths from xxxxxxx Basic Skills centre (next door to the Co-op in Broad Street, open 9-5 Mon-Fri, Sat am)	15 Feb
If you can't get an Apprenticeship, go to the Midtown College's reception centre and apply for either the motor vehicle programme or Entry to Employment. Ask to speak to the motor vehicle tutor, Chris Turner.	28 Feb
Gary to phone me (Jo) if you get stuck with any of this.	Any time
Jo will contact Gary again if I have not heard from you.	1 March

Signed...........*Jo Bloggs*......Adviser   Date......... .21ˢᵗ Jan........

Signed.......*Gary Smith*........ Client   Date..........21st Jan........

PART 2

THE GUIDANCE INTERVIEW - DIGGING DEEPER

Sometimes you will find that by following Bedford's seven stage model you have only scratched the surface for the client. You have given them the information they asked for, but this is not enough. They are not enthusiastic about taking up the ideas you have suggested and you can tell that you have not met their needs.

So what can you do? How can you help further?

If you are advising clients about Learning and Work (Education, Training and Careers), it could be that your client needs a deeper level of help known as Guidance.

What is Guidance? How is it different from Information and Advice?

INFORMATION

In the context of learning and work, information giving is described in "Information, Advice and Guidance for Adults: The National Policy Framework and Action Plan" (DfES/LSC/Ufl, 2003) as:

> "the provision of information on learning and work, without any discussion about the relative merits of the options"

and in "The Challenge of Change" (NAEGA, 2003) as:

"providing information about learning opportunities and related support facilities available, without any discussion about relative merits of options for particular clients"

ADVICE

These two documents go on to describe advice as:

"(it) requires more interaction with the service user, usually on a one-to-one basis. It may require explanation of some of the information provided, how to access and use information, and a recognition of when more in-depth services may be required by the user." (DfES/LSC/Ufl, 2003)

"helping clients to interpret information and choose the most appropriate option. To benefit from advice, clients must already have a fairly clear idea of what their needs are." (NAEGA, 2003)

If you have been carrying out the basic helping interview as described in Part 1, you are likely to have been delivering information and advice.

GUIDANCE

Your client may need more than information and advice if...

- He does not have a clear idea of what he wants or where he is going
- She says she has a clear goal but does not take any action to achieve it
- He has a number of concerns, each affecting the other (money, relationships, etc)
- She has a number of barriers to entering and maintaining learning or work, including lifestyle issues

In 2003 the English government department for Education and Skills (DfES, 2003) described guidance as helping clients to:

- "understand their own needs relating to learning and work"
- "set and review goals/objectives for learning and work"
- "understand their barriers to learning and work"
- "overcome barriers/obstacles to learning and work"
- "produce learning and career action plans"

NAEGA, the National Association for Educational Guidance for Adults, has become part of CDI (Career Development Institute). It defined guidance *(NAEGA, 2003)* as a combination of seven activities:

1. Informing
2. Advising
3. Using counselling skills
4. Assessing
5. Enabling
6. Advocating
7. Feeding back

Another definition describes guidance as:

" using counselling skills to bring about change in clients' thinking or behaviour" (Bimrose et al, 2004).

COUNSELLING SKILLS

The basic interview as described in Part 1 focused on informing and advising, which may have included some forms of assessing and enabling. In this Part 2, we will look at the help you can provide in the one-to-one situation through the use of counselling skills.

To provide a model for this more in-depth means of helping, we will refer to the work of Gerard Egan. Egan wrote "The Skilled Helper" in 1975, and it has been constantly in print ever since. This book is written for helpers offering counselling in a range of settings. It gives a model for problem-solving which can be understood by the client as well as being used as a guide or structure by the practitioner. He calls it a client-centred model, using the ideas of Carl Rogers to underpin his approach.

Since the NAEGA definition of Guidance added "using counselling skills" to "informing" and "advising", Egan's model can be used by guidance practitioners even though guidance is not quite the same as counselling.

Egan (Egan, 1994) sees the process of helping as going through three stages. He calls these:

"Stage 1 – Reviewing the current scenario
Stage 2 – Developing the preferred scenario
Stage 3 - Getting there"

Put into more everyday language, we can explain these to the client as:

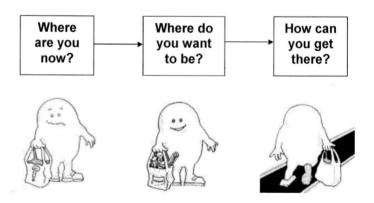

Guidance is concerned with all three stages of Egan's model. The model reminds us that there is no point in helping a client with the third stage (planning how to get there) if he does not yet know where he wants to get to (second stage). He may not even fully know where he is now, so Egan's model encourages us to start by exploring the client's "current scenario".

Building a working alliance

As the research done by both Tol Bedford and Jenny Bimrose has shown, clients are not going to discuss their hopes and fears with us unless they trust us and feel at ease. So before we launch into Egan's first stage, you still need to built a friendly, supportive relationship and to clarify the contract for your work together, as in your advice interview, see Part 1:
1. Create a friendly, encouraging atmosphere
2. Agree the purpose and boundaries of the interaction

Exploring

'Explore' is a very important word in guidance. It suggests that we spend longer on Bedford's activity 'Gather information from the client' to help the client look beneath the surface and beyond the presenting question, to find out what really are the issues and concerns with where she is now, and to build a picture of the future she would like.

The Toolkit section of this book will suggest a range of ideas for helping a client explore. The tools are designed to explore in two ways:

1. Help clients understand themselves (develop their self awareness) ... **Who am I?**

2. Help them decide how they want to fit into the world ...
   Where do I want to be?

They can also look at how their values will shape the goals ...
<u>Who</u> do I want to be?

You will find a number of books proposing a four-stage model for career guidance interactions. Two models (Ali and Graham, 1996 and Kidd, 2006) use a similar approach to Egan's, incorporating a fourth stage at the start - clarifying and building the relationship.

Returning to Egan's three stage model, in Guidance you will be helping a client work out:

Where am I now?	Where do I want to be?	How can I get...
• Who am I now?	• Job/Career	...from here -
• What can I do?	• Lifestyle	• Where I am now
• What interests me?	• Relationships	...to there -
• What are my values?	• etc	• Where I want to be

Egan suggests that to get from one stage to the next, we need to take the client through three sub-stages. A paraphrase of his model (Egan, 1994) is:

Where am I now?	Where do I want to be?	How can I get there?
a. Help Client tell their Story	a. Consider a range of options	a. Consider various strategies
b. Identify and challenge any blind spots	b. Choose some options to turn into goals	b. Choose best fit strategies
c. Prioritise what to change or work on first	c. Commit to these goals	c. Make a step-by-step plan

Egan's Stage 1 – Where are you now?

If a client is choosing a career or a course of further study, looking at what they are good at now (their SKILLS) and what they enjoy now (their INTERESTS) will provide useful pointers to the kind of learning and careers they will enjoy and in which they will be successful in the future.

Telling the Story – Egan's Stage 1a

In helping the client tell their story about their skills and interests, you will use the methods discussed in Part 1, especially those for Step Three: Gathering Information. You can ask about their career to date, what they have enjoyed most and least, what feedback they have had. Feedback could be in the form of verbal praise, through promotions, qualifications gained, pay rises, bonuses, or via appraisals. If they are just at the start of their career, you can ask about favourite school subjects, exam grades, how they choose to spend their spare time. If they bring you a CV or if you have given them a form to complete in advance of the interview listing their career and education to date, you can ask them to talk you through it telling you which parts they enjoyed most. Some advisers use the narrative approach – they ask very few questions but sit back and listen as the client talks about themselves, taking the story wherever they want.

Lifeline – Timeline

If the client does not provide you with their career or educational history, one technique that can help them open up and explore what they have enjoyed is to draw a simple timeline. Mark points along the line, perhaps the decades (when they were 10, 20, 30 and so on). Then ask them to mark times when they felt particularly content or successful, and ask what was happening in their life at that time. See Part 3 for an example of a timeline.

Interest Inventories

There are a range of questionnaires asking people what they enjoy or would enjoy in a job. Most of these are now computer based, although paper based ones still exist. Some can then be scored according to types, for example Holland's six career types: Realistic, Investigative, Artistic, Social, Enterprising and Conventional (described in more detail in Part 3). Jobs and careers can also be classified into these six types and the client can be shown careers that might be of most interest to them. (Holland, 1973)

Other interest inventories produce a list of career suggestions that most closely match with the answers given by the client. These can be very useful for people who want some ideas, although they are often more useful if an adviser is at hand to guide them in the use of these, because they can be misleading and lead to a disappointing set of ideas which then de-motivate the client.

There are a number of computer-based questionnaires that help clients identify their interests and link them to job and career ideas. Some are free such as "Skills Health Check" provided by the government at:
https://nationalcareersservice.direct.gov.uk.

Your organisation may choose to subscribe to others such as Cascaid's "Adult Directions" (or "Kudos" for younger clients) or "Prospects Planner" available at www.prospects.ac.uk.

Career Types

The case on the next page shows how you can use the six career types suggested by Holland without necessarily using a questionnaire. After listening to the client describe the activities they most enjoy (in work, school, home or social situations), you may start to see a theme emerging that links closely to one or two of the Holland themes, and you can then tell the client what you have noticed, describe the types to them, and see if they agree.

James was uncomfortable in his managerial role. He was leading a large team, involving issues such as discipline, performance and motivating people through a period of change. As he talked about what he had enjoyed best in his career, he mentioned ensuring the budgets were accurate, designing computer programs to perform certain tasks, planning and organising the department's activities.

At home he was very organised, with a place for everything and everything in its place; he enjoyed stamp collecting and gardening; he planned interesting and unusual holidays down to the last detail. His adviser reflected back to him how all these preferences seemed to link more to the Conventional theme than any other, possibly with some of the Investigative theme. There was not much evidence of an interest in the Enterprising theme which would enable a person to deal more robustly with the team manager's job of influencing people and making difficult decisions.

James began to see that he would be more comfortable managing projects, finance or IT rather than managing people.

Abilities

To discover the client's strongest skills and abilities, you can of course ask what they have achieved academically. Their qualifications are likely to show the level they have achieved and also the subject areas (ie: verbal, numerical, scientific, practical skills, mechanical, artistic, etc) that they find easiest.

Skills Audit

Clients will know their own strengths and weaknesses. You can encourage them to list all their skills and rate them. The book 'Build your own Rainbow' (Hopson and Scally, 1999) provides a set of cards each with a different skill, which can then be classified into four main types. There are also computer questionnaires that lead to identifying strengths in the same four areas:

- Data
- Ideas
- Things
- People

You can help the client use the "Skills Health Check" (https://nationalcareersservice.direct.gov.uk.) which provides a skills audit to get a similar breakdown of their skills.

Testing and Assessment

Asking some clients about qualifications and school may be a painful reminder of past failures, and some people's exam passes do not reflect their true ability. If you have a client with dyslexia or whose first language is not English, their written or spoken communication may not reflect their capabilities.

There are many skills and ability assessment tools available to measure where a client is now, so that you know how to build on his skills to help him move towards where he wants to be. In your job role and organisation, you may be able to access some of the basic skills assessments to find out a person's level of literacy, numeracy and IT competence. If you do not have access to these, you may be able to refer the client to someone who is qualified to administer them.

There are psychometric tests to measure reasoning ability (these used to be called IQ or intelligence tests but now it is more usual to assess intellectual reasoning and problem-solving via aptitude tests, looking at how quickly people can solve complex problems rather than testing their knowledge). These tests usually have to be administered either by psychologists (occupational or educational) or by non psychologists who are on the British Psychological Society's Register of Qualifications in Test Use.

Educational psychologists may also be qualified to use more specialised tests to diagnose the various difficulties that may be a form of dyslexia, and to assess reasoning ability without results being skewed by dyslexia.

EQ and IQ

Daniel Goleman, in his book 'Emotional Intelligence', highlighted the fact that being clever or intelligent is not sufficient to succeed in most work roles. The ability to understand and get on with people is of equal if not greater importance. So, when assessing a client's abilities and aptitudes, it is important to help them to value their interpersonal skills, so they understand what personal strengths they can bring to any team or workplace: You can encourage them to seek feedback, for example appraisals in some organisations rate people according to sets of desirable behaviours, such as: Respect for Others, Self-Confidence, Teamwork and Co-operation, Planning and Organisation, Effective Communication, Negotiating and Influencing, Coaching and Developing Others, Political Awareness.

Personality Profiles

Psychometric assessments of personality can be used (use is normally restricted to suitably qualified practitioners) for an indication of an individual's ability to demonstrate these behaviours. Some well known personality instruments are the Myers Briggs Type Indicator (see Part 3) and Cattell's 16PF (16 Personality Factors). There are many different assessments in use that your clients may come across, including Belbin's Team Roles (see Part 3).

360° Feedback

360° feedback involves asking those who work with the individual to rate that person on a set of characteristics, and then using the feedback to help the individual understand the impact they have on others. This feedback can increase their self-awareness which they can use either to make changes, or to accept who they are and choose work roles that play to their strengths. This technique is fairly widely used in organisations. It should be carried out in a structured, professional and sensitive manner, preferably by someone trained to use a standardised instrument, since it is clear to see the harm that could result from clumsy use.

Probing blind spots or misconceptions – Egan's Stage 1b

As you listen to the client telling her story, you may think that parts of it sound unlikely. Is she really as low skilled as she thinks she is? Is it always someone else's fault that things don't work out for her? Did her lifestyle have nothing to do with failing exams and getting sacked from jobs? Is it true that people like him can't do jobs like that? Going through some of the exercises above, you may already be helping the client see themselves in another, more realistic light.

Challenging

We return to challenging in Egan's Stage 2, but at this first 'Where are you now?' stage, the challenging is if anything more difficult, because you are challenging the client's self-image. You could do a lot of damage here if you are not extremely sensitive, but if you do not challenge blind spots, you are not going to be able to help the client move forward and make the changes she really wants to make. There are certain phrases we tend to use in making gentle challenges, for example:

> "You say .... but ...."

> "On one hand you say ..... but on the other hand...."

> "I'm getting a mixed message."

> "You say you are doing all you can to save money, but you've just booked a holiday."

> "You are applying for all these jobs, you do really well in interview, but each time you are offered a job you turn it down."

or ...

> "You tell me ..... but the way you have been working with me, I see something different".

> "You say you are desperate to do training, but you have not followed up on any of the courses I've told you about."

> "You say you are well organised and efficient, but you've been late for every one of our appointments."

> "You say this does not upset you, but you look rather tearful."

This latter technique is known as immediacy. Read more about Immediacy and the Art of Challenging in Part 3.

Prioritising what to work on first –
Egan's Stage 1c

If the client has told you about lots of issues, you may wish to narrow down and focus, and choose one that is key.

Clients may have several requirements or needs, perhaps too many to deal with all at once, or some more important than others.

Egan sets out some principles for the setting of priorities. Even if you think other issues are more important and need to be dealt with in order to solve the client's difficulties, deal first with:

- An immediate crisis
- Part of the problem that is causing the client particular pain or distress
- An issue the client perceives to be important and is willing to work on
- An issue which, once resolved, could lead to a general improvement in other areas
- A problem which can be dealt with without requiring more effort or investment than the client can give

As always in client-centred advice and guidance, we can probably get the best answer from the client. You could use questions like:

 # LACK OF TRANSPARENCY

Transparency is a key factor that is easy to overlook. Some passive or trusting clients may not want to know why we asking questions as we encourage them to tell their story, but others could be suspicious or uncomfortable if they do not see why we are probing into their personal lives. Think about it: how do you feel if you don't understand why a professional is asking or acting in a certain way? Ever felt like that with a doctor or lawyer? Taken to an extreme level, this could be perceived as abuse of power.

Making the process obvious to the client will help you gain their trust and engagement in the process. Explain what you are doing, and why, linking it to their presenting issues:

"I need to ask you this because..."
"The reason I am asking is..."
"We will need to discuss...because..."

Egan's Stage 2 -
Where do you want to be?

A mix of the exercises and ideas above should help your client understand who and where they are now. Discussing these will also have started them thinking about where they want to be. This is when they need to make some decisions.

Most of us approach decision-making in a variety of ways, not always rationally (see The Decision further on in this chapter). When working with clients, it is helpful to have a model in mind, to encourage them to take a rational approach, thinking through all the issues. This will reassure us that the options they choose will be right for them. We have found this model helpful:

Define the Question
What are you deciding about?
This has just been agreed at the end of Egan's Stage 1

Clarify the Issues
VALUES - What matters? What is this for?

Generate Options
Consider a range of options
Egan's 2a

Assess the Options
Choose one/some option(s) to turn into goal(s)
Egan's 2b

Choose and Commit
Commit to achieving the goal(s)
Egan's 2c:

Clarify the issues – Values

Perhaps the issue of values should be the first consideration when helping a person to understand who they are and who they want to be. Some people value winning, others value supporting; some value material success, others value creative success; some prefer the commercial world, others the academic world. Whatever their skills or the activities they enjoy, they will not be happy using or doing these in the wrong setting for them.

Values are not always easy to identify or describe, but they provide the motivation for everything we do: work, study, social activities. Our values are the basis on which we make all our choices and decisions.

Would we all provide the same answer to this question? Do you:

Work to live? --------------or-------------- **Live to work?**

The question highlights a basic difference in the way people see their careers. Most people have a mixture of the two work values, but it is useful to find out where a client stands on this when you are helping them choose between career options.

Live to work suggests you need a career that is right for you as a person, a job that reflects your personality, skills and values. Some people use their work to express themselves and to achieve their potential. They need to believe in what they do.

Work to live suggests you prefer a job that will give you what you want to live the life you choose, that is (depending on your needs): money, status, family-friendly hours, the right geographical area. Some people prefer to keep their interests and passions separate from their paid work. Some people are unable to find paid work that could interest them and match their personality, and will look to family life, friends, hobbies, community involvement and/or spiritual life to develop and express their true selves.

You can present people with a list of values and ask them to rate them; such lists can be found in career choice or self help books.

'Build your own Rainbow' (Hopson and Scally, 1999) provides an exercise using a set of about 40 cards, each with a different value written on it (eg: making a lot of money; helping people; helping society; independence). You are asked to sort these to arrive at a set of eight top values. You then look at any careers you are considering and rate them against those values.

Yasmin had excellent communication skills and loved writing. She thought she wanted to be a journalist.

Her top values included Creativity, Helping Others and Family Life. On thinking about journalism again, she found that she would probably have to begin by writing about local events, court cases and council meetings. She would need to be available at all hours if a story broke, and to progress she would probably need to move to London, taking her away from her children. She also felt she would be helping the newspaper proprietor more than helping the less fortunate in society.

She looked again at her choices and decided to use her skills as an English teacher. In her spare time she could write articles on topics she believed in, novels and plays, providing an outlet for her creativity and not compromising her values.

Maslow's Hierarchy of Needs

Psychologist Abraham Maslow (Maslow, 1987) said that our values are based on our needs. People are motivated to act in order to meet or satisfy a need. To understand a client's values, the adviser must identify which needs are driving him. Maslow, like Rogers and other humanistic psychologists and therapists, believed that all humans have a drive to reach their full potential, which he called self-actualisation. However, this drive cannot function if basic needs have not been met. He developed his theory into a hierarchical model, with the lower ones having to be satisfied before the person can attend to those higher up.

Self Actualisation
Drive for
self-fulfilment,
achieving full potential.

Esteem
Self-esteem and the
respect of others.

Love and Belonging
To belong and be accepted.
To give and receive love and affection.

Safety
To feel secure and safe from harm.

Physiological
Survival: Water, Food, Shelter, Oxygen.

Personal Constructs

If you feel a client has his own set of values which you have not been able to identify through the usual values exercises, you can try another method. Peter Beven (Beven, 1995) and Marcus Offer (Offer, 1995) introduced us to the idea of using Kelly's Personal Construct Theory (Kelly, 1991) in career guidance. This is a different and more client-centred way of finding out what guides a person's choices, rather than matching him against a set of pre-conceived categories (such as Holland's six career types or Hopson and Scally's set of work values).

First ask him to write down the names of about six or eight jobs or careers he thinks are good. Then ask him to list a number of less desirable ones. Next, ask him to take two from the good list and one from the bad. He should then say what the two good ones have in common, and what makes the bad one different. Note down the words he uses to describe the good ones. Then, ask him to reverse the process, taking two from the bad list and one from the good, and again say what the two bad ones have in common and how the good one is different. If you repeat this process a number of times, you will arrive at a list of features which, in the client's view, constitute a good or a bad type of career. This may help you and the client understand what drives him, what his values are in relation to work and jobs.

Another way of using this exercise is described in Part 3.

 # OUR OWN VALUES

It is generally accepted that it is good for the country's economic and social wellbeing for us all to be educated, employable and productive. If you work in the field of learning and work, there is a strong possibility that you share this view. However, you will have your own personal opinions on all kind of related issues, your own values. How much should we pay for childcare? Should single mums work? Should benefits be withdrawn from the work shy? Should all training be free? We are all entitled to our opinion, even if we don't agree with each other.

The danger here is that we assume our clients share, or should be made to share, our own values. We need to be careful that we do not try to impose ours, or our organisation's, on the client. They may hold different values, for reasons of their own. Finding out what is important to them is part of helping them make decisions. Maybe we should question them if they are not thinking constructively – but we have to accept that it is not our job to make them the same as us.

At the age of sixteen, Teresa decided to marry and have children while she was still in her teens, go to University while her children were finishing secondary school, then have a teaching career uninterrupted by babies. And that is exactly what she did. Not all life choices go according to plan, but this one did. If she had been your client at sixteen, how would you have handled her?

If you are not clear what your personal values are, go and work it out, because you need to know. Then consider how they may impact on your practice with clients. You can try for yourself the techniques and tools we suggest for clients.

Generate Options –
Egan's Stage 2a

Let the client start the ball rolling

Remember that your client may already have thought of several options for himself, and because we are aiming to empower clients to take control of their own lives, we will only move in to make suggestions if we think they have not considered all the possibilities. Start by asking a question like: "So what have you already thought of?"

Evaluate

As you listen to their ideas, you can assess how much they know about the options available to them, and how far their choices are taking into account what you have learned about who they are now (their abilities, interests, values). Tol Bedford (Bedford, 1982) used the mnemonic FIRST to remind advisers of five questions to help us evaluate the clients' ideas about where they want to be:

- **Focus:** how far has the client narrowed down the options to a set of ideas that appear to be coherent and linked, or does he appear to be flitting from one disconnected idea to another?

- **Information:** do the client's ideas appear well informed, or are they based on misconceptions about what is possible?

- **Realism:** how realistic are the options in relation to the client's resources and how the world works?

- **Scope:** do you think the client is too focused too soon, without considering all the possibilities?

- **Tactics:** (this relates more to Egan's stage 3 – Strategies) Does the client know what action to take to achieve their goal?

Make Suggestions

If you think the client needs to broaden his **scope** and look at a wider range of options, you will make suggestions, helping him to generate more ideas. In making suggestions, you will be using the skills and techniques covered in the Part 1: Stage 5 – Provide Information to the Client.

Information

To make suggestions, you need to be well informed. Informing is one of the seven activities of guidance listed in "The Challenge of Change" (NAEGA, 2003). This is where you can tap into your own particular area of expertise, which is what brought the client to you for advice in the first place. You will know what information resources you can access, and you will know the importance of continually updating your knowledge, to keep it current, accurate and comprehensive.

 BIAS - DELIBERATE OR ACCIDENTAL

We strive to be impartial and unbiased, but we need to be aware how easy it is to unduly influence our clients. If we have more knowledge in one area than another, have recently been influenced ourselves by a presentation from an employer or provider, or just have more enthusiasm for one option because it matches our own interests, we run the risk of skewing the client's decision making process. We also may have areas that we avoid discussing due to our own insecurities or lack of experience. Can you identify options you enthuse about and options you would rather not address?

Realism

Giving information to clients about the options they have thought of (and suggesting new ideas) is a way of giving them a more realistic view of what they could achieve.

If you are showing them they have more options than they hoped, they will probably welcome this new view, although they may be overwhelmed by it.

If you are giving information that puts barriers in the way of their hopes and aspirations, you may need to help them handle their disappointment. You will need to be very sensitive in the way you present the information to them, and creative in finding ways round the apparent barriers.

Darren was a qualified chef who had his own restaurant. Although it was successful, profit margins were not high. Now he was married with one child and another on the way, his wife was not able to earn and the family needed more money. He wanted to train as a primary school teacher, as he enjoyed training his apprentices and helping in his son's nursery school, and he knew teaching offered a regular, secure income.

When he explored this option with the careers adviser, he learned that he would have to train for three years on a student loan which would then need to be paid back.

In helping him come to terms with this disappointment, the adviser put forward the idea of teaching catering in a further education college. He could train as a teacher of adults via a part time evening course, so he could carry on running his business until he was qualified, and slowly build up his teaching hours. This compromise would allow him to reach his goal of teaching without taking an unacceptable risk.

Challenge

If you spot inconsistencies or gaps in the clients' knowledge of the real world, you will be gently and appropriately providing any information they need to encourage a realistic choice. You may also be pointing out any inconsistencies that they have overlooked:

> ➤ You did say that you are a vegetarian, have you thought how that would feel if they asked you to work on the meat counter?

> ➤ You told me you are very shy, but now you say you'd like to be a receptionist. How would you cope with meeting all those people?

You may learn that they have in fact thought it through and they can explain their reasoning, or you may help them to evaluate their ideas more thoroughly and work towards a more realistic option. Read more about the Art of Challenging in Part 3.

Assess the Options – Egan's Stage 2b

Having generated as many options as possible, encouraging the client to think creatively and widen their scope as far they can, the time has come to narrow down again. She will need to make some decisions and choices.

In Career Guidance, the client needs to assess the possible options against her:

Skills

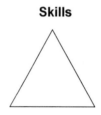

Interests   **Values**

You have helped the client identify all three of these in the work you have been doing in Stage 1 and the early part of Stage 2.

To help her measure these (herself) against what is available to her (the opportunities) you might try:

- The Values exercise in 'Build your own Rainbow' (Hopson and Scally, 1999)
- PMI scan: (a kind of Pro's and Con's list)
- SWOT Analysis: her Strengths and Weaknesses for this option, and the Opportunities and Threats this option presents to her.

Read more about these in Part 3.

The Decision – Identify the Goal –
to complete Egan's Stage 2b

Now the client should be able to make a decision and choose a goal to focus on, whether it be choosing a career, deciding on a course, or making a decision about how to tackle a financial, health or personal problem.

You have tried to help the client weigh up the pro's and con's of the various options in order to choose the most suitable. This would amount to a rational or logical means of decision making.

Occasionally clients seem not to be so rational in their decision-making and Gerard Egan agrees that:

> "in actuality, decision-making in everyday life, and in counselling, is not the straightforward rational process.... it is an ambiguous, highly complicated process .... confused, covert, difficult to describe, unsystematic and at times quite irrational. Many, if not most, of the decisions that are made every day are based not on reason, but on taste." (Egan, 1994)

Other theorists have identified the different styles we may use at different times in our decision making. This can help you assess how a client is making decisions and if necessary point out to them any potential pitfalls in their method. Some of the decision-making styles that theorists have identified are:

- **Rational**: planned, researched, logical, carefully thought through, taking personal responsibility for the decision

- **Intuitive**: taking personal responsibility for the decision, but more reliant on feelings and inner experience, based on a sense of it feeling right

- **Emotional**: based on subjective preferences or feelings, impulsive

- **Hesitant**: unable to make decision, therefore postponed

- **Compliant**: based on perceived expectations of others

- **Dependent**: Denial of personal responsibility for decision, or projection of responsibility on to others

You need to be aware of your own preferred decision-making style and take care not to impose it on the client. Be aware that no one style is always right for everyone or for every situation. However, you may sometimes need to raise a client's awareness of their style, and in some cases encourage them to think more rationally or logically.

Specify a Goal –
Egan's Stage 2b finalised

The aim of stage 2 is to decide on a goal. This may be a specific career goal:

> ➢ I have decided I want to be a Farmer, a Graphic Designer, a Hairdresser.

It may be a more general work goal:

> ➢ I have decided I want to work in a warehouse, in an office, with children.

Goals can be set in any area of life:

> ➢ I want to clear all my debts
> ➢ I want to move into my own flat.

SMART Goals

Clients who came to you not knowing where they were heading will probably be very satisfied with having identified a goal. However, there is a world of difference between identifying a goal and achieving it. In order to check out whether the client can commit to the goal, it is important to define it thoroughly and check that they understand what it really means. As we mentioned in Part 1, S.M.A.R.T. gives us a checklist in articulating the goal for the client. If you can send a client on their way with a goal that has been described in Specific, Measurable detail, that Appeals to them, that is Realistic and Achievable and is set with Timescales, he now has something clear to work towards.

Examples of SMART goals:

- By the time I am 21, I want to be a qualified Hairdresser, having completed an apprenticeship and working in a salon in town. This appeals to me because I am creative, good with my hands, I enjoy meeting people and I like fashion. It is realistic because I am likely to achieve the necessary grades to be accepted on the college course and I will have the support of my parents while I train on a low wage.

- I want to aim for career progression in human resources. I would like to be in a HR assistant's post one year from now. This appeals to me because I like law and administration and I want to work with people but not to the extent of social work or other helping professions, preferring the business environment. It is realistic because I have a business studies qualification and I have worked in administration for several years.

- I want to lose at least one stone and get back into the suits I bought when I got married. I would like to do this by next summer when I finish my degree course and will be applying for jobs. It is appealing because I want to look good and save money on clothes. It is realistic because I know people can achieve this level of weight loss and I have the support of my wife who is also slimming.

See Part 3 for more on SMART Goals.

Commit to the Goal –
Egan's Stage 2 c

As stated above, there is a still a long way to go between identifying a goal and achieving it. Forming a clear action plan (Egan's Stage 3) will help, but Egan suggests that we consider some of the barriers to commitment at this stage as we help the client specify their goal. Sometimes clients find it difficult to move from theoretical goals to action. Egan suggests that you need to establish:

Appeal: The goal must be appealing or attractive: it is more appealing to aim to get something rather than to give something up. To get into size 12 clothes is more appealing that to give up eating chocolate. Appeal can also be the **A** in **SMART**.

Ownership: The goal must be set by and belong to the client. It must fit the client's value system, rather than that of the helper or some other person.

Competing Agendas: Barriers must be taken into account, and planned for. Clients may have to set priorities, perhaps giving up certain conflicting demands on their time and energy, or accepting that they do not have the resources to achieve all their goals while these demands exist.

If you feel a client is not committed to achieving the goals agreed on, you may need to challenge. You could do this by asking a question such as:
- So this time next year, where do you think you will be?
- What will be different then from how it is now?

You may then learn what is stopping the client from seeing the new goals as realistic, and be able to work on the issues.

PROJECTING OUR LIMITATIONS

Just because you would never face violent situations or be a steeplejack, you don't have the determination to get a PhD or the guts to bungee jump, don't assume your client can't. Your limitations are yours, not theirs.

Egan's Stage 3 –
How can you get there?

Egan divides this activity into 3 stages:

A. Consider a range of **possible Strategies**

B. Choose **Best Fit** Strategies

C. Make the **Plan**

Stage 3 includes two types of Action Planning: a long-term plan for sub-stages A and B and a short-term "to-do" list for sub-stage C.

Consider Possible Strategies –
Egan's Stage 3 a

Egan suggests brainstorming (some people prefer to call this activity a thought shower) to help the client see there could be several ways to get to their goal from where they are now.

He warns us against advice-giving. Rather than tell the client what we think they should do, we can present clients with information, such as:

> ➢ Here are some things other people have tried.....what do you think?

In guidance for learning or work, we could show the client careers information, describing various routes into a career.

In the learning pack "Developing Adult Guidance Skills" (National Extension College, 2001), Rosemary Jolley suggests two types of long-term action plan that you can draw up to help clients look ahead and understand the different routes they could take to achieve the same goal:

The Route Map and The Year Plan

The Route Map can help a client see what needs to happen and in what order. For most objectives, there is more than one way to achieve it, so you may draw several of these plans, to help a client compare and decide which is the most suitable method for them. A route map can also show how the plan could be altered, depending on level of success at one stage, or on changing circumstances.

Below is an example of a route map to help a client consider a range of strategies (there are more routes, not listed here):

Where she is now: mother of two young children, aged 35, a care worker with NVQ level 2, and GCSEs at grades D-E.

Where she wants to be (her **goal**) is to become a registered nurse:

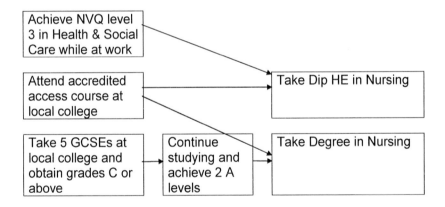

The Year Plan for the same person. This shows how one of the routes would fit in with the rest of her life:

This Year*	Next Year*	2 years time*	3 years time*	4 years time*
Start access course at college, apply for DipHE courses	1st yr of Nursing Dip HE course	2nd year of Nursing Dip HE course	3rd year of Nursing Dip HE course	Start work as qualified Registered Nurse
Elder child in infants school, toddler with childminder, both with childminder in holidays	Elder child in infants school /after school club, younger child in nursery school/with childminder, both with childminder in holidays	Elder child in infants school /after school club, younger child in nursery school/with childminder; both with childminder in holidays	Elder child in junior school, younger in infants school, both to after school club; still need child care for holidays	Elder child in junior school, younger in infants school, both to after school club; still need child care for holidays

*To make the plan more meaningful, you would write in the actual years.

104

Choose Best Fit Strategies – Egan's Stage 3b

Anticipate Difficulties

There are many reasons why action plans may not lead to action. There are psychological barriers as well as material ones. While you do not want to de-motivate the client by listing all the potential barriers, there are ways we can help the client to think in advance what could prevent them achieving their goal, so that they can plan ways around these barriers.

SMART

Check that each strategy is:

- **Realistic**: does the client have the resources (ability, strength, stamina, support, finance) to achieve it?
- **Acceptable**: does it fit the client's values?
- **Appealing**: to motivate the client to put in the effort required?

Force Field Analysis

The aim is to help the client identify the **restraining forces** (what might prevent them taking the action they are planning), and plan how to decrease them, and then how to increase the **facilitating forces** (things that can help overcome that barriers).

John's goal is:
"I want to achieve higher grades than predicted for my "A" levels."

Restraining forces are:

- my inability to organise my revision time
- Pete and Tom who want me to go out every evening
- no table at home to spread out my books
- my part-time job (need money)

Facilitating forces are:

- a revision programme offered by my school
- Jo and Mike who are studying too
- the public library or school library, or a friend's house
- parents might give me more pocket money

Part 3 presents two diagrams for presenting force field analysis visually to a client.

Sampling

Some people do not find it easy to visualise in the abstract to consider whether they would enjoy something or what the dangers might be. They need to try something for real before they really understand what it means to them

You might think of ways for such clients to try out some of the options before deciding to commit. For example by:

- work shadowing
- work experience
- visiting
- volunteering

Making the Plan –
Egan's Stage 3 c

Rosemary Jolley (National Extension College, 2001) calls this type of plan a **Plan for Immediate Action**.

Why do you need a plan? Egan (Egan, 1994) says, to:

- Help clients develop the **discipline** required to achieve their goals
- Keep the steps towards goals **bite-sized steps**
- Help clients **evaluate the realism** of their goals, by seeing how much action they require
- Raise awareness of the **resources needed** to implement the plan
- Reveal potential **pitfalls and barriers**

What should the plan look like?

Egan identifies four requirements:

1. **Activities** - identify the specific activities needed to achieve the goal or sub-goal

2. **Sequencing** - put the activities into order: 1st, 2nd, 3rd, etc..

3. **Deadlines** - Give each activity a time frame or target date

4. **Anticipate Difficulties** - and ensure the client has a strategy for dealing with them, even if this is only to return to you.

Rosemary Jolley suggests a list of six elements:

1. **Priorities** (order) of actions, with timescales

2. **People** the adviser and the client must contact

3. **Information** to aid access (addresses, appointment times, phone numbers)

4. **Key questions** to ask

5. **Action** to take once answers have been found

6. Arrangements for **reviewing progress**

An example of a plan for immediate action has been provided in Part 1 – Stage 7: Clarify Next Steps.

Having gone through Egan's 3 stages, you hope you have helped the client identify a realistic goal that he really wants to achieve, and plan the steps necessary to get him there.

Job Done!

PART 3
THE TOOLKIT

Getting the Full Picture
- SWOT
- PMI Scan
- Offa's Agenda
- Scales

Decision Making
- Turn the Tables
- De Bono's Six Hats
- Force Field Analysis
- Takeaway
- Honey's Four Options

Changing Perception
- Plan Your Escape
- Blank Page
- The Other Boots
- Helicopter Vision
- Change Curve

Challenging
- Pussyfoots and Clobberers
- Immediacy
- Three Stage Perception Checking
- Holding up a Mirror
- Steering
- First Impressions

Positive Thinking Techniques
- Replacing the Tape
- Visualisation

Expanding Horizons
- Brainstorming
- Mindmapping
- Lateral thinking
- A to B via D
- Pot of Gold

The Heart of the Matter
- Mirroring
- Six Category Intervention Analysis
- What makes you say that?
- Timeline

Build them up, Buttercup
- Aardvaarc
- Find the Spark
- Sales Talk
- Expectancy
- SMART Objectives

Learning/Coaching
- How we Learn
- GROW Model
- Kolb's Learning Cycle
- Learning Styles

One size fits all? Type and Career Theories
- Jung and Myers Briggs
- Belbin's Team Roles
- Holland's Career Types
- NLP Categories
- Personal Construct Theory
- Super's Rainbow
- TA – Are You My Mother?

Tools and Techniques to try for different difficulties with clients

Looking for a shortcut to save you reading the whole book? Here are some suggestions for tools that may help with different types of situation or barrier clients present in the guidance interview. Of course they are not prescriptive, they are just ideas that have worked for us. There is no substitute for your own experience, which will increasingly build your confidence and skill in assessing a client's situation accurately and finding the way to help them overcome their barriers and move forward.

Biased Clients
- Holding up a mirror
- SWOT
- PMI
- Force Field Analysis
- What makes you say that?
- Brainstorming
- Mindmapping
- Offa's Agenda

Dithering Clients
- Scales
- Steering
- Pot of Gold
- Takeaway
- Force Field Analysis

Victim Clients
- Replacing the Tape
- Visualisation
- Aardvarc
- SWOT
- The Other Boots

Down on themselves Clients
- Positive Thinking techniques
- Plan your Escape
- Helicopter Vision
- Replacing the Tape
- Sales Talk

Jump in Too Quick Clients
- Lateral Thinking
- Six hats
- Offa's Agenda
- What makes you say that?

Non responsive Clients
- Immediacy
- Find the Spark
- Change Curve
- Mirroring
- Timeline
- NLP Categories

Negative Clients
- Six Hats
- SWOT
- Changing Perception
- Positive Thinking Techniques

- Visualisation
- PMI Scan
- Pot of Gold
- Find the Spark
- Change Curve

Stuck in a Rut Clients
- Turn the Tables
- Positive Thinking Techniques
- Visualisation
- Pot of Gold
- Brainstorming
- PMI Scan

Unrealistic Clients
- SWOT
- Force Field Analysis
- SMART Objectives
- Holding up a Mirror

Getting the Full Picture

Let's face it, you are unlikely to be able to move your clients forward if you don't know where they're currently at. They often need help to see it clearly for themselves too. Sometimes clients make the job easy by volunteering all the information you need in order to help, but more often than not you need some techniques to draw out the full picture. There can be different reasons for this reticence. Maybe the clients just do not recognise the significance of some things, or they would rather forget difficult matters like failing at school. They may be shy, embarrassed, uncomfortable with the present situation....and then they can be very adept at coming up with a crucial fact just as they are leaving and time is up. So here are a few techniques that will help you dig out what you need to know. We call them scanning tools, because they can give you an overview of what is going on with your client. Give them a try.

SWOT

An old favourite that has been used in business and training for years, a SWOT analysis can have a place in one-to-one work. Basically it is a 2 X 2 grid where you map key issues under the headings of Strengths, Weaknesses, Opportunities and Threats.

Here is an example:

Strengths	Weaknesses
Good with people	Inconsistent work history
Okay GCSE grades	Health issues
Quick to learn	No driving licence
Office/admin skills	Rusty office skills
Opportunities	**Threats**
Major new employer coming to town	Restricted by school hours
Free courses at the library	My own self esteem
Support from Jobcentre Plus	Need a good wage to come off
More free time now the children are at school	benefits
	Currently have no good references

Once you have got this far, you may need to reorganise the lists in order of importance, or limit the length of each list by choosing the top three or four issues so that your client isn't overwhelmed. Now you have a useful tool that will help your client see the situation clearly and they will probably be able to come up with action points. You should be focusing on how to maximise strengths and opportunities, address the weaknesses and limit the impact of threats.

PMI Scan

This is one of Edward De Bono's tools (De Bono, 1994), similar in principle to SWOT: a simple framework you can remember easily. PMI stands for Plus, Minus and Interesting. It's pretty self explanatory – there are elements in most situations which are pro's and cons, but De Bono also encourages us to look for the interesting factors, those that make a situation unique. These may be around the skill set of the individual, unusual experiences that they have to draw on, their interests, unusual approaches....you get the drift.

Offa's Agenda

Clients arrive with agendas – their presenting issues, thoughts and concerns. There is always a danger in taking this at face value, and an even greater danger of attempting to help our client without realising the significance, depth or importance of aspects of their story. Offa's Agenda is a simple model that breaks down the components we need to explore to make sure we discover, to the best of our ability, a realistic understanding of their position. If you can remember the acronym, you have a framework for exploring with your client.

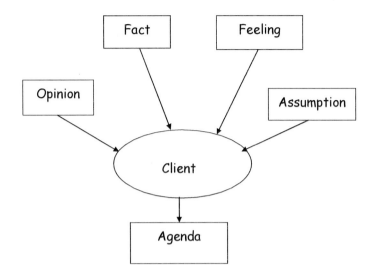

Take, for example, the client who wants do a course but won't go to the local college because, he says, the teaching is rubbish, no one ever passes exams and the staff are unhelpful. What is he basing his opinion on? Is he making assumptions based on limited information? You can sometimes alter perception by giving information, which in this scenario may be showing him statistics on pass rates, talking about staff you know personally, or mentioning the successes of other clients. We are all entitled to have an opinion, but it's important that we shed light so clients realise if they basing their opinion on unsound criteria. It takes skill to do this without either party becoming defensive, which can easily happen if someone challenges what we believe to be true.

The Feeling category is interesting too, requiring us to suspend our own thoughts on the emotions we would expect clients to attach to parts of their story. Most of the time we can guess the range of feelings that are likely to be attached to events, eg: we are nervous before interviews, happy to be promoted, etc, but now and then you will find a client who does not present the emotions you would expect. It is important that we get a handle on how the client feels, or it can render any action plan unworkable.

Scales

Clients are often unintentionally vague about their aspirations, which makes it hard to know how to help them or assist them with prioritising. Much of our role is to help them get clarity of thought – many thinkers say that understanding the problem is 80% of the solution. Most experienced advisers have developed ways of getting through the fog by separating out the issues and asking clients to quantify them in some way. One way of doing this is to create a series of scales to help build up a comprehensive overview.

To do this, you need to think what would be at either end of the scale, and then ask the client to say where they are now and/or where they would like to be. It can also be useful to help them identify a band they think is acceptable.

Say, for example, you have a client who says they want to get back into office work, thinks their computer skills are rusty, is worried about interviews but wants to start earning again. There is a real danger here of going into automatic pilot when giving solutions because it is such a common scenario.

You could, however, break it down into the following scales:

| 1 | 2 | 3 | 4 | 5 | 6 | 7 | 8 | 9 | 10 |

Doesn't want to work ---Desperate to work

Can't switch a PC on ----------------------------------Expert at Microsoft Office

Terrified of interviews -------------------------------------- Brilliant at interviews

Destitute -- Plenty of spare cash

After discussion, your client might score the scales like this:


```
1     2     3     4     5     6     7     8     9     10
Doesn't want to work                         Desperate to work
-----------------------------------------------------X-----------------
Can't switch a PC on                         Expert at Microsoft Office
-------------------------------------------X---------------------------
Terrified of interviews                         Brilliant at interviews
-------------X---------------------------------------------------------
Destitute                                         Plenty of spare cash
---------------------------------X-------------------------------------
```


In which case, priorities become apparent and you will be able to start planning action accordingly. But what if the client scored the scales like this?


```
1     2     3     4     5     6     7     8     9     10
Doesn't want to work                         Desperate to work
-----------------------------------------------------X---------------
Can't switch a PC on                         Expert at Microsoft Office
--------X--------------------------------------------------------------
Terrified of interviews                         Brilliant at interviews
-------------------------X---------------------------------------------
Destitute                                         Plenty of spare cash
-----X-----------------------------------------------------------------
```


In this scenario, the need for money overshadows other concerns, and the interview may well progress to finding a stop gap measure of other work to make ends meet while the bigger plan is worked on (See A to B via D). This example is of course a simplification of a client's problems, but it does demonstrate the importance of quantifying the issues.

An example of a tool available commercially that makes the use of scales accessible to clients who prefer the active, hands-on, kinaesthetic (see NLP categories in Part 3) approach to communication is The Rickter Scale® (see bibliography).

This describes itself as a "non-paper based assessment and evaluation tool... for engaging individuals in motivational solutions-focused work... in a non-threatening and non-judgemental way".

It is based on a board with a pointer than the client can move up and down a scale. On the board you can place one of a series of overlays each asking a set of questions about a particular topic, for example:

On Preparation for Work, questions include:

> ➤ How important to you is having a job?
> ➤ How certain are you about the type of work you want to do?
> ➤ How important is it to you how much money you earn?

On Life, the questions explore feelings about:

- Employment/Training/Education
- Accommodation
- Money
- Relationships
- Stress
- Confidence
- Health

Decision Making

Turn the Tables

This is a useful technique to help clients find a different way to think about how to solve their problems. It can be fun, but you would need a good rapport with your client to see it through. It also works well with groups. There are three steps:

1. Ask the client to describe the very opposite of what they want to achieve. For example, they may dread being trapped in a dead end job, so they might talk about being bored every day, increasing frustration, not being able to afford luxuries, etc. Keep going until you both have a clear picture of the scenario.

2. Ask them what they would need to do to make sure this really happened. Compile a list of their responses. It may include things like "I would need to....never look at other job ads; believe I'm not capable of more; stay away from anything that might teach me new skills, etc". See the example on the next page.

3. From there it is a simple step to turn the tables by reversing the list, which will give you good start on identifying what needs to be done. Don't do this for the client; instead help them to work it out for themselves. Give the client time to take on board the results before you begin prioritising and action planning.

How To Stay In This Rut:	Turn the Tables:
Keep my head in the sand	Be alert and look for opportunities
Don't look at job ads	Buy the local papers, check out agencies, find the job centre on the internet
Make sure I don't learn new skills	Check out the local college and evening classes. Choose something I'll enjoy
Be resigned to never having my own home	Set my sights on having my own space, visualise what it would be like
Don't accept new challenges or more responsibility at work	......And so on. How would you help your client finish this list?
Keep telling myself I'm useless	
Be scared of failing	
Avoid anyone doing a college course	
Lose my out of date CV and certificates	

De Bono's Six Hats

Edward De Bono (De Bono, 2000) has produced many strategies to encourage productive thinking. His work is well worth checking out, particularly if you want to encourage your clients or learners to develop their thinking skills. We've seen Six Hats used effectively in interviews, in training sessions, and also as a means of keeping lively team meetings in order. Imagine six hats, each of a different colour. Each represents a different style of thinking as below:

Virgin White
Pure Facts, Figures and Information

Seeing Red
Emotions and Feelings, also Hunch and Intuition

Devil's Advocate Black
Problems and Difficulties, Negative Judgements, Why it will not Work

Sunshine Yellow
Positive and Constructive, Optimism, Opportunities

Fertile Green
Creative, New Ideas Springing from Lateral Thinking, Provocation

Cool Control Blue
Overview, Summaries and Conclusions, Orchestra Conductor, Thinking about Thinking

To make sure you help clients to effectively weigh up their options, or even their current situation, take them through each hat. You can do this showing the client a visual aid (we have a handout with all six hats on), by telling them verbally about the six hats, Cor you can just use it as mental checklist for yourself to make sure you have the ground covered. If you are aware that a client is prone to not seeing the full picture, for example they always return to the doom and gloom aspects, it can be useful to have a visual aid so that they can see what they are missing. For groups, we sometimes use laminated A4 sheets with a different hat on each. Once they know the framework, you can just hold up a hat, for example yellow, and the group can only contribute positive comments on the topic under discussion.

Force Field Analysis

Many business books will give you a more detailed account of how to use this tool, but a simple version can be used easily with clients, scribbled on a sheet of paper as you talk. It is a tool to help with decisions, by weighing up the forces pushing you towards an option (facilitating forces), and those pulling you away from it (restraining forces).

Write down the issue at hand vertically down the middle of the paper. This example is 'Taking the factory job'. On the left hand side, draw arrows pointing to the middle and label them to identify the forces that are pushing you towards a course of action. Try to make the size of the arrow reflect the size of the issue, so if getting a wage packet is a major factor, draw a big arrow. On the other side, predictably, you do the same with factors pushing you away from the course of action. Think of it as being like a tug of war!

Example

Take the Job   **Don't take the job**

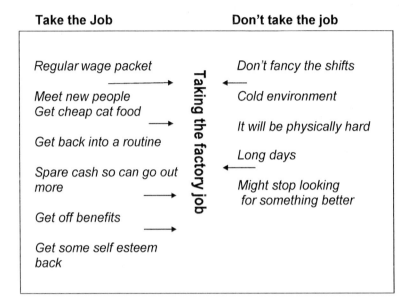

Regular wage packet   Don't fancy the shifts

Meet new people   Cold environment
Get cheap cat food
                                   It will be physically hard
Get back into a routine
                                   Long days
Spare cash so can go out
more   Might stop looking
                                       for something better
Get off benefits

Get some self esteem
back

Taking the factory job

From there, you can begin to get a sense of whether the option is viable. There is still work to be done; you can look at the diagram and talk through the arrows on both sides. Are there activities that will strengthen the driving forces? Can the detracting forces be lessened in any way? Or can the client's perception of them be changed? Help him by exploring the factors with him, and make any amendments he suggests.

Force field analysis can also be used in action planning, to anticipate any barriers or potential difficulties that might prevent the client putting his plans into action. See Part 2 for an example.

A simpler way to present this method to clients could be through the **fishbone** image. This one uses the example from Part 2.

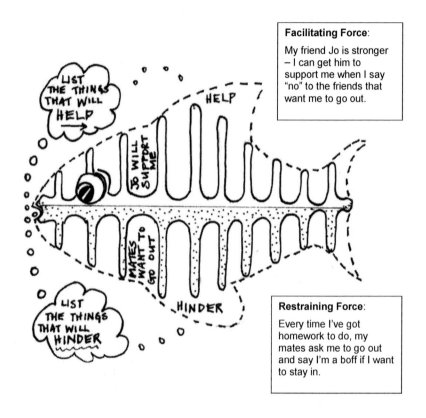

Facilitating Force:

My friend Jo is stronger – I can get him to support me when I say "no" to the friends that want me to go out.

Restraining Force:

Every time I've got homework to do, my mates ask me to go out and say I'm a boff if I want to stay in.

Takeaway

If a client is finding it hard to decide between options, a simple trick that can shed light is to write the options on separate pieces of paper and lay them in front of the client. Then take one away and ask the client how they feel if this option is removed. Repeat with every option to get the full picture. This can be surprisingly effective.

Honey's Four Options

According to Peter Honey (Honey, 1988), we have four options with any people problem. As advisers, we have two ways of using this concept; we could use it ourselves to help us think through the client's options, or we can introduce it to our clients so that they can use it to help sort their own issues. Passing on easily digestible models like this one to clients can be exceedingly useful to them, as they can store them away for future use. The options are:

1. Do nothing

Useful if it is an informed choice – ie: you have weighed up all the options, considered all factors involved, and come to realise that any other action will leave you in a worse position than you are now. If you are helping a client and this is the decision they reach, it may well also help change their perception too. It may be a 'pick your battle' scenario; the issue is best left as it is because there are other weightier things (the war) to address. It can also be liberating to know that doing nothing is an option!

2. Change the situation

We get conditioned to act in certain ways in some situations, so our feelings and behaviour may be formed before we even enter, and they carry through. We can look for the triggers that set off the behaviour and feelings, and find ways of changing them. You probably remember times when even a change in the environment (new office, more space, brighter colours) has made you feel differently. Even small changes can be effective. Have you had clients who say they hate their job? Sometimes they do. Other times, you will discover that the job role is actually right for them – it is the circumstances, or situation that they dislike, such as a bad boss, poor working conditions, unpleasant colleagues, etc. These present a very different scenario requiring different solutions.

3. Change your perception

Changing clients' perception can be critical in advice and guidance work. There are tools to help you do this in the section below, but many of the other tools that help the client see the full picture will lead towards perception change. You may need to change your own perception, because you will unconsciously deliver what you think. If you think that compiling statistics is a waste of time because it takes you away from the clients, which is the real work, you will always associate negative feelings with it. If, however, you see it as the essential hard evidence that brings in funding because it proves the worth of your role, you may feel differently. If you have taken them through the process described in Part One most clients will change their perception in some way.

4. Persuade the other person to change their behaviour

This is the hardest option. It can be done, but some of the skills used by effective influencers do not sit comfortably with the ethics of one-to-one work (for example manipulating emotions, offering rewards, withdrawing privileges) so we need to carefully consider our tactics. See the section below on visualisation techniques – if you can get your client to describe how they want their life to be, it's a logical step to think about the behaviour that will lead towards this. Also see the Challenging section – because it is no use asking a client to change their behaviour if they do not know how.

5. The Fifth Option

Of course the fifth option, which is implied in three of the above, is change your own behaviour. It's can seem a last resort if you are doing it in desperation without knowing how it may impact – but if what you are doing isn't working, you have little to lose by behaving differently. A good strategy for our own reflection and development is to try and identify our behavioural style, think through other approaches that are feasible in the situation, and then consider where they may lead. Self awareness is a crucial skill for anyone involved in one-to-one work, if we are to have any understanding of how we affect others. There is more about this, or rather the lack of it, in The Dangers – Lack of Self Awareness in Part 1. Say you are usually a warm, friendly person who presents in an unhurried way, and you have got into a rut with a client who turns up every week and goes through the same motions but never moves forward. What difference would it make if you came over as more brisk and business like? Or more prepared to challenge them? This is not asking you to become artificial, rather to explore your own repertoire of behaviours and maybe extend your comfort zone round the edges.

Changing Perception

Changing the perception of the client is often a product of guidance, whether it is planned or emerges naturally from the process. As our aim is to move our clients forward, expanding or developing their thinking is one of the most important elements. How can we get them to think about their situation differently? Below is a collection of tips, some of which you are probably already familiar with.

Plan Your Escape

Let's face it, in most sectors, we advisers speak our own language. Maybe it's not as alienating to the clients as some forms of technobabble, but it surely isn't motivating. Talking of Action Plans and SMART objectives will make many eyes glaze over. Some words and phrases, however, strike chords with individuals. With experience, we find out what works. This is a good example. Say you have a client who feels totally stuck in their position and sees no way out, and you say "Right, let's plan your escape". What could this convey? Maybe:

- ➤ There is a way out
- ➤ I'm not in this alone
- ➤ There's light at the end of the tunnel
- ➤ I've taken the first step

...and so on. The client begins to reframe their perception, and starts to see that there may be a way out. This may not work for all stuck-in-a-rut clients, but it will help change perception for some.

Blank Page

A similar technique to Plan Your Escape, this is also just an easy choice of words that can help clients to shift their thinking. It is helpful for clients who are embarrassed by their lack of qualifications or experience, and perhaps view themselves as in deficit. "So, we're starting with a blank page...", followed by words or phrases that suggest....

> ➢ I can make a fresh start
> ➢ I can choose what to put on the page
> ➢ Failure in the past does not have to affect the future
> ➢ It's up to me. Life is what I make it

.....which is significantly different from focusing on what they haven't got.

The Other Boots

Many of us use this already, but maybe we don't use it to its full potential. It is a method of getting clients to think about their issues from a different perspective, by asking them how they think their actions/behaviour seemed to others involved in their story. There is a place for this with clients where nothing is ever their fault, or who view another person's actions negatively.

How would it feel to be in the shoes of the boss that fired you, the interviewer that rejected you? How did you respond to them? How did that make them feel? What rules were they bound by? What impact did your behaviour have on them? Ideally, you should keep going until they fully understand a different viewpoint, but this is not always necessary or appropriate. You run the risk that this approach may just entrench their feelings of injustice, so handle with care.

Helicopter Vision

If a client (or an adviser) is worried about a specific issue, the stress can cause us to over focus on it and get it out of proportion. The issue can become a real block to progress if we can't see beyond it.

Take the client who slaves away trying to get a job interview, and is then unsuccessful, or the one who invests a lot of money in a training course that they don't pass. Ask them to describe the situation to you, allow them to construct a complete image. Then ask them to imagine they are looking down on the situation from the ceiling.

What do they see? Describing it from outside is the beginning of being objective about the situation. Once they have done this, ask them to move upwards, looking down on perhaps the whole building.

What do they see now? Maybe other people struggling with the exam, other people waiting to be interviewed, who also aren't successful. If they go even higher, what enters the scene? Maybe hospitals, schools, all kinds of people dealing with their own problems and lives.

Ultimately, if you looked down from high enough, what then? The aim is to get a sense of perspective, an objective assessment of the size of the problem when compared to the whole picture, and to be able to see beyond it.

This is another tool that not only can be used in an interview, but once learnt, the client can use it themselves to help counteract stress.

Change Curve

The majority of clients reach advice and guidance services because they are facing change of some kind in their lives. They may want change, but more often it seems that they have had it thrust upon them.

People may appear to respond to change in different ways, but usually they have gone through the same emotional stages. You can help clients understand the stages of change, to show them that the feelings they have, such as frustration or depression, are a natural part of the change cycle. It can be very liberating for them to see their progress through the curve.

Elisabeth Kubler-Ross (Kubler-Ross, 1997) developed this model, mainly through her work with the bereaved. It has been found to be relevant to many situations where change is occurring, since change often involves some form of loss, even when we have chosen it willingly. In advice and guidance for learning and work, our clients may be facing change and loss as a result of leaving school or college, redundancy or departmental re-structuring and staff changes. In other areas of advice work, people may be facing other types of change and loss: for example their home, their good health, their freedom. It is important to realise that people move through the stages at varying rates, and spend differing lengths of time at each stage. To be able to help others, we must:

- Understand the stages
- Be prepared for inconsistency between individuals
- Have strategies to support clients through the perceived difficult stages

Change Curve cont'd...

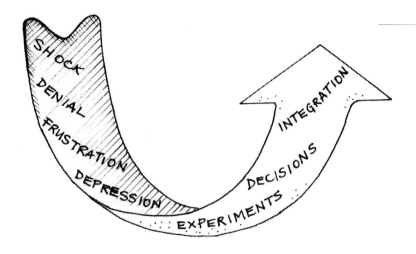

1. Shock or surprise - it can't be true

2. Displaying ostrich tendencies - if I stick my head in the sand and ignore it, it will go away and I can carry on the way I have always done

3. Anger and frustration - why me?

4. Depression and apathy - feelings of being helpless, lack of self confidence, not being able to see a way forward

5. Looking for a way forward to bring ourselves out of the depression and apathy

6. Deciding how to accept and implement the change - beginning to see a way through it

7. Successfully integrating the change into your work or life

Challenging

There are times when we want to challenge our client. Reasons may include lack of realism, lack of co-operation, unconstructive behaviour or attitude, contradictions, distortion, assumption, blinkers, seeming unreasonable….we could make a long list.

We need to handle this sensitively if we are not to lose trust. If we are not careful, we could do a lot of damage to the client's self esteem and to our relationship with them. However if we notice blind spots and do not question them, we are not going to be able to help the client move forward and make the changes s/he really wants to make.

In Part 2 we have already mentioned some phrases we tend to use in making gentle challenges:

> I'm getting a mixed message from you.

> You say .... but ….

> On one hand …..................... but on the other hand….

> You tell me …....................….. but the way you have been working with me, I see something different.

Gerard Egan (Egan, 1994) recognises that as helpers we will find challenging difficult. He feels it is better to be reluctant to challenge than too eager, and that challenging should be done sparingly and with great sensitivity, although once we have decided to do it, we should do it assertively. He gives us some important principles:

• Always challenge for a specific reason, with a specific goal in mind, don't be vague

• Give the client ownership by helping them challenge themselves (eg: "If we swapped roles and you were me, what would you say to yourself right now?")

• Only challenge once you have created a safe environment for the client, by building a supportive relationship, showing unconditional positive regard for the client

• Be tactful and tentative, but not apologetic

- Challenge clients to be aware of their strengths rather than their weaknesses
- Remember to keep challenges within the client's own set of values, do not impose yours on him

Another counselling trainer, Richard Nelson Jones (Nelson Jones, 2000) offers some suggestions too:-

- Offer your challenges as an equal, and avoid talking down to the client
- Allow clients to decide whether or not to agree with your interpretations
- Only challenge occasionally, otherwise you risk creating an unsafe emotional climate

A challenge may lead to a breakthrough that can feel like a great relief to you, the helper, but which may come as a bombshell to the client, especially because they are the one who has suddenly seen things differently. One of us recently had this exchange with a client:

Helper: "What would you say to yourself if you were me?"

Client: "I'd say to myself: 'You're burying you head in the sand, you're refusing to face the facts even though they are staring you in the face. The fact is no one else can help you with this. You've got to take action yourself'."

Helper thinks "Yesss! At last!"

BUT this is not a competition, and at this very moment the client is at his most vulnerable. We aimed to show very little emotion but to remain still and calm, with a body posture that reflected care, support and interest: sitting for a moment, saying nothing, feeling supportive and caring, and also impressed with that courageous self-revealing honesty. Then perhaps a minimal encourager such as "really?" or "do you think so?". Possibly then an invitation to say more, such as "Go on…" or "what action could you take?".

To challenge effectively, we would suggest the two qualities you need most are:

- assertiveness - having the courage to say what needs to be said
- sensitivity - putting care of the client before any other consideration.

Pussyfoots and Clobberers

It is of no use to make clients aware when they are thinking or behaving unproductively unless we can help them to find a better way. How would you like it if you were told that you were using a new gadget wrongly, without being told the right way? To challenge without helping clients to find a better way is doing them a disservice. Of course, any kind of challenge, however sensitively put, can evoke an emotional response in the client.

We need to avoid the two extremes: to pussyfoot or to clobber. We have even seen advisers swing rapidly between the two, pendulum style. You can imagine the frantic thought processes going on: aware that they have been too hard and then over-compensating by backing off too far. You need to find the middle ground. The most critical thing of all is to allow the client space to deal with your words. Don't rush them.

This adaptation of Heron's model (Heron, 1989) depicts the process well:

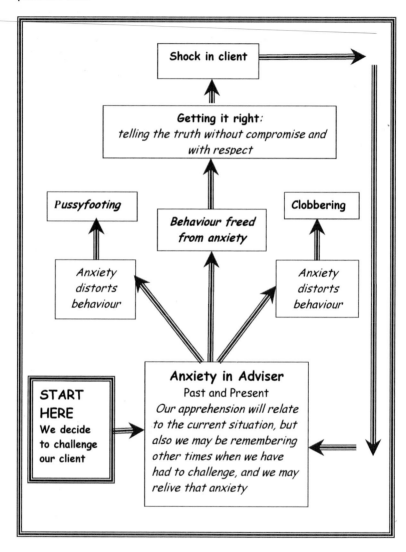

Immediacy

There is little more frustrating for an adviser than conducting a seemingly textbook interview, only to have a gut feeling that somehow the client was only going through the motions. This can happen because the client has not really bought into the process: maybe they are attending because another agency or person thinks they ought, or maybe they have other issues in their life that are higher priority, thus commanding their attention.

(Egan, 1994) suggests we develop the skill of immediacy to use in circumstances where we feel the client is not engaging effectively. Immediacy means addressing what is going on between you and the client in the here and now, rather than the issue they have come to discuss. So you might say "It seems to me that you have something else on your mind. Do you want to talk to me today?" Honesty about how the client's actions are affecting you can have a place too. "I'm finding it difficult to talk to you when you seem so agitated". If you have an ongoing relationship with a client, seeing them more than once or twice, it is all the more important that you address any difficulty with the communication between the two of you.

Three stage perception checking

This is a remarkably effective technique that is best used to nip unwanted behaviour in the bud, but it can also be used for immediacy to clarify the state you think your client is in. It works because it addresses and makes transparent behaviours that we often passively choose to ignore. The stages are:

1. Identify the behaviour
2. Say what it means to you
3. Ask for confirmation

For example, you might say:

> ➤ You've been drumming your fingers constantly since you arrived (Stage 1)
> ➤ I take it that means you are in a hurry to be somewhere else (Stage 2)
> ➤ Am I right? (Stage 3)

Or:

> ➤ I see that your hands are shaking (1)
> ➤ Often that is a sign of stress (2)
> ➤ Are you worried about talking to me today? (3)

Holding up a Mirror

If we held up a metaphorical mirror, would our client recognise themselves? Reflecting back is an important guidance skill, but when we are faced with a client who needs to have clearer view of themselves, we need to do more than just reflect back their words. Holding up a mirror is a form of challenging; what can we do or say to help the client see themselves as others see them? We may need to ask them what impression they think they are creating, or how they think others will interpret their attitude, or reflect their ideas and arguments back more than we usually do. There are times when the best thing we can do for the client is help them increase their self awareness, so that they are better equipped to deal realistically with the world and the barriers they may face.

Steering

Given opportunity, many clients will talk about anything and everything – for some, access to a good listener is a rare treat. Others will avoid issues or subjects that may be uncomfortable to discuss, or that they feel may not portray them in a good light. This poses a dilemma for the adviser; how do we keep them on track so that the task at hand is accomplished? Or is it sometimes more useful to let them unload? You need to make your own judgement, but at times you will need to steer the conversation without alienating them. Visually, think of it as bundling up the off-track topic, acknowledging it, putting it to one side and then turning back to the job in hand. Here are some tips:

- Reiterate time boundaries
  - ➢ We only have 20 minutes left...
- Remind them of purpose
  - ➢ You say you need to discuss the costs?
- Acknowledge the subject matter.
  - ➢ I can tell your journey was a nightmare.......... but we should get back to your problem
- Refocus on the identified need
- Ask if it is relevant. Sometimes it is, but we can't see the link.

First Impressions

What does this diagram tell us?

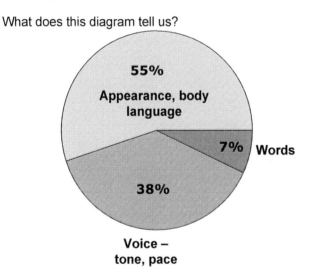

Albert Mehrabian (Mehrabian, 1971) is famous for research on communication, and for coming up with the well used and misused statistic shown in this pie chart. He discovered that others gain messages from us about our attitudes and feelings based on the impact of our appearance, our voice and our words, in unequal proportion, as shown in the diagram.

This could influence the way we prepare ourselves before we meet colleagues or clients. We need to ask ourselves:

- Are we fully aware of the impact we currently make on others?
- How can we judge ourselves on each area (appearance, voice, words)?
- Do our behaviour and appearance support each other?

As well as recognising our own impact, there are times when we need to help our clients understand how they may be perceived by others, particularly if they are preparing for interview or are concerned about joining other students on a course. Sharing information, such as this piece of research, can be an effective way of challenging. Also bear in mind, as we said earlier (Part 1 – Congruence), that if there is dissonance between appearance / body language and the words spoken, it is the body language that will be believed. At the very least, if there appears to be some discrepancy between the messages being sent, the other person will hear alarm bells ringing.

Positive Thinking Techniques

What difference would it make to our clients if they believed in themselves? Clients have enough challenges to contend with in the big wide world, but often too they have other barriers that are internal. Unintentionally they may have convinced themselves that they will fail again, let themselves down, or be unable to learn. Life's harsh lessons may have entrenched these thoughts. Many people have written about the power of positive thinking and having a PMA (positive mental attitude). We probably use some of these techniques ourselves, but it can be really beneficial to pass them on to clients, especially those who struggle with self esteem or have had many knock backs, so that they can help themselves on an ongoing basis. Of the many variations on this theme, the work of Anthony Robbins (Robbins, 1997) can be a good place to start. A few techniques are described below, all requiring discipline and repetition to work effectively. Once the methods are firmly lodged in the brain, they can be recalled when required with ease.

Replacing the Tape

Now and again we can identify messages that are ingrained within the client, that they may have been programmed to tell themselves for years. Often they started in youth, with labels that we continue to wear without considering whether or not they are still justified. Stereotypically it is teachers or parents who say things like "You'll never amount to much". Experiences such as this eat away at confidence and impede our ability to move ourselves forward – sometimes it's easier to retreat than to put yourself in the firing line. Of course, if your client has substantial problems with negative thinking, it is likely to be outside your remit or skills to help them and you may offer to refer them for more intensive support such as counselling. However, there are few people who cannot benefit from learning to control their thinking.

We can think of the negative message as a tape that our brain plays over and over. This begins to help by positioning the tape/thought as something that is not an intrinsic part of our makeup. If we mentally remove the tape, we can replace it with another tape that plays a better message, for example "I am a bright, confident woman with a lot to offer". Every time you find yourself playing the old tape, imagine taking it out and putting the new tape in. There are many variations on this theme. Most writers agree that the unconscious delivers what the conscious thinks, aka the self fulfilling prophecy, which is why it is so important to make our thoughts constructive. Of course our subconscious has long held beliefs programmed into it that are not going to disappear the first time we make the effort to change the tape. Persistence is the key, until the subconscious accepts the new tape. Ayd Instone, in a challenging essay about self esteem, says if you look in a mirror every day and say "I like myself", it takes 21 consecutive days before your subconscious gets the message. Don't knock it until you've tried it.

Visualisation

We can use visualisation techniques to help with motivation, positive thinking, breaking bad habits – all manner of issues that our clients, and we ourselves, have to grapple with at some stage in our lives. They work by giving us a clearer view, at the forefront of our consciousness, of what it is we are trying to achieve. We know the importance of action planning, but it can be hard for clients to get to grips with how their lives will change if they carry out their plans, particularly if they are worried or nervous about changing their lives. We may recognise that the status quo needs to be changed, but it is difficult to leave the familiar comfort zone that we know so well for a future that is hazy to us.

- If you are enabling your client to think about what it will be like to achieve a goal or take a course of action, ask them to describe a picture of what it will be like. Take time to help them get as much detail into it as they can. You can use the five senses to do this – what will it look like, sound like, feel like? You may struggle with smell, but you get the idea; you are working towards a complete picture that the client can engage with in many ways.

- Use colour and size. NLP practitioners (see Neuro-Linguistic Programming further on in this section) use techniques like this one. If a client is trying to replace a negative with a positive, for example being more confident at interview, or even getting out of bed on time, ask them to visualise the unwanted behaviour in glorious technicolour, on a screen as big as they can view. Do the same for the wanted behaviour – a big, bright representation of how they want it to be. Once they have done this, go back to the first picture and ask them to visualise it fading in both colour and size, becoming paler, then black and white, then paler and smaller still, until it is miniscule. Then imagine the second picture bursting onto the screen to fill the space. Do this several times, so that a firm link between the pictures is established

- Robbins recommends fixing a physical anchor or prompt to help you bring back the second picture. For example, as you do the exercise above you could pull on a finger or squeeze your wrist. Keep it up until you reach the point where squeezing your wrist automatically brings the big, bright, positive picture to mind.

- Another approach, the type sports people often use, is breaking it down into stages and walking through each stage in your mind. It is good preparation for situations like interviews, races, speaking in public or exams. This has two fold benefits; it both helps you to think positively and rehearses you for the event so that you are more prepared.

Expanding Horizons

Often we go round in circles, or reach dead ends in our thinking. It is hardly surprising, because we only have our own resources (knowledge, thinking style, experience, drive) to draw on. There are times when we need to find fresh approaches for our own growth and development, and we need to help our clients climb out of the ruts they find themselves in too. Finding ways of generating options is essential to advice and guidance work. Even if there seems only one feasible option, it is good practice to help a client explore alternatives because it is empowering. If you take the only option, it feels passive, like Hobson's Choice. If you feel you have chosen the option, having considered the alternatives, it becomes a decision you can feel ownership for.

Brainstorming

Brainstorming (sometimes now known as wordshower or thoughtshower) is a tried and tested tool for generating options. It involves suspending judgement and just coming up with as many options as possible, without regard to how feasible, promising or completely outrageous they are. Once the list is generated, you can then begin to whittle it down. It can be a methodical exercise, but it also can be challenging once you begin to unravel why some ideas are dismissed. Clients may have to face and reconsider their own preconceptions, or add new ideas to their thinking. It has remained a popular technique because often a seed of a new approach is found among the chaff.

Mindmapping

Mindmapping was developed by Tony Buzan (Buzan, 2002) as a way of thinking through and developing a topic. This tool can be used simply, or by following Buzan's instructions, it can become much more thorough and complex. For use in one-to-one work to support discussion, the simple approach probably fits the bill. You may have also come across similar tools known as spidergrams or bubble charts which work along the same lines. This is another way of adding a dimension to your discussion by organising thoughts on paper. You simply put the topic in the centre of a sheet of paper, and draw lines out from it to represent ideas, thoughts, areas that need exploring etc. You can then branch off the lines to subdivide them or link areas with dotted lines. Once you have exhausted the topic, you can make sense of the mindmap by prioritising areas and listing action points. Many people use these regularly, and can write essays, plan projects or deliver speeches directly from the mindmap.

Mindmap example

Lateral thinking

Edward De Bono coined the phrase 'lateral thinking' to describe thinking more broadly. He has devised many concepts (such as Six Hats and PMI, described above) to help us improve our thinking skills. His books contain many simple exercises to help us flex our thinking muscles, some of which will be useful for work with clients, and others that help us learn for ourselves how to think more productively. One such technique is Blocking the Route. This means when we have tunnel vision, or do things the same old way from habit, we should first identify the predictable behaviour (eg 'I always get jobs through the Jobcentre' or 'I always work in shops'). Imagine you are on a road, and in front of you, the route is blocked. You have to take a fork to divert you from your usual habit: if you cannot do something the way you usually do, what alternatives are there? Where might the fork lead if the road to the Jobcentre is blocked?   Or if you cannot work in a shop?

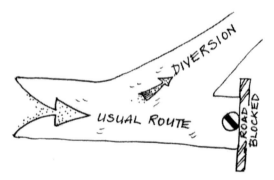

A to B via D

The journey analogy often works well, and can be used in many ways. Often there is not a direct route from where we are to where we want to get to – from A to B – so we need to take a longer route to get to our destination. What stops might there be along the journey? If a client cannot do the training they want because of finance issues, the journey may need to go via ways of earning extra money or saving. It is important that the client can see that even if they cannot progress exactly as they would wish, the end destination can be achieved, albeit by a scenic route. Sometimes it works well to draw this along a line (which may not be straight!) so the client can see the route. The section on Action Planning (Part 2) describes this process further.

Pot of Gold

There are many variations of this tool, but they are all similar so we have grouped them here. The basic principle is to help the client see through their obstacles and current circumstances and discover their ideal future scenario. Ways of doing this include:

- Imagine you find the Pot of Gold at the end of your rainbow. In it is everything you want to achieve. What is in it?
- Miracle Dream - If you fell asleep, woke up and all your problems had disappeared, what would you be doing? BUT... see Danger! (below)
- North Star - What would be your ultimate aim if you could reach for the stars?
- If I waved a magic wand......
- If you did know the answer to your problems, what would it be?
- Draw me a picture of a day in your ideal life – visual and kinaesthetic clients (see NLP categories below) will probably prefer to literally draw this rather than use just words.

You can probably add more to this list. To be effective, you need to spend a little time setting the exercise up so that client understands the purpose and is engaged enough to be able to share their dreams with you. You, on the other hand, will need to be focused. It is easy to digress and start talking about a problem the client mentions, especially if you can see the solution – but if you do this, the exercise drifts away, incomplete. If this happens, the thing to do (see Steering) is to acknowledge the problem, say you will return to it, and carry on with the exercise, reminding the client of the process and aim if necessary.

In guidance for learning and work, it is likely that there will need to be some discussion about what is holding the client back from their dream, and then an appraisal of which obstacles can be removed, and which need to be endured or worked round. However, the technique can help clients understand themselves better, which in turn can increase motivation. It also, paradoxically, can make clients more realistic about their personal barriers.

 ## TAKE CARE WHEN OPENING THE BOX

Advisers who use the "Miracle Cure" or "Magic Wand" type of technique find it helpful because the process often reveals important aspects of a client's values or thought processes that have not been discovered in other ways. Beware the dangers that lie within, though. You should frame this exercise within the boundaries of your role, so the question may be: "What is your ideal job/training course/home…?" rather than "What is your ideal life?", or you could find yourself swamped with information that is way outside your remit and that you do not have the skills to support the client in dealing with the issues this raises.

We are warned by Dr Hazel Reid (Reid & Bimrose, ed, 2006) that "an inadequate understanding of the theoretical underpinnings (of counselling techniques) can lead to the practitioner using a technique without the resource to deal with the consequences." She gives the example of using the "waking up to find all your problems solved" question with a client who has lost a parent or whose criminal record or medical condition presents a barrier to many careers: their answer may present more serious issues to an adviser without the skills, time or other resources to resolve them.

The Heart of the Matter

There are times when we just can't get to grips with what the client is saying. It may be because they use language differently to us, or perhaps they are saying what they think we want to hear, they are worried about revealing something or just don't express themselves clearly. Sometimes there is a lack of understanding just because they are very different to us, making it hard to find a connection. Whatever the reason, we will need to understand them in order to help, which means we must find a way of probing to the heart of the matter.

Mirroring

You are probably familiar with mirroring – which means echoing the other person's body language with your own – as a way of creating rapport. Close friends do it automatically, you can observe this unintentional ritual in any busy bar or restaurant. However, NLP-ers (see Anthony Robbins) take this a stage further. They say that if you want to understand better where another person is coming from, try emulating their posture, breathing, tone, pace – in fact anything you can observe. The theory is that these observable traits are outward signs of our inner state, so by experiencing similar outward behaviour, you can make progress towards understanding how the client is feeling. It is easy to imagine how mirroring could destroy rapport if done clumsily, so don't attempt it unless you feel confident and you've honed the skill outside of the interview room.

Six Category Intervention Analysis

Occasionally an interaction is ineffective because the dynamic between the client and adviser isn't working too well, and we need to find a different way to interact. John Heron's (Heron, 1989) theory reminds us that we have a choice in how we respond to a client. With experience it becomes easier to choose the most appropriate responses, but we all have a favoured style that is comfortable to us, and need to be prompted to step out of automatic pilot now and again. The Six Category Intervention Analysis is also a very useful framework to use when we reflect on our work. We can consider which types of intervention come most easily to us, which are most fitting in our work role, and which we should develop skills in. The categories are:

Authoritative

1. Prescriptive
Seeks to direct the behaviour of the client, usually referring to behaviour that occurs outside of the client-adviser relationship

2. Informative
Seeks to impart knowledge, information, meaning to the client

3. Confronting
Seeks to raise the client's consciousness about some limiting attitude or behaviour of which they are relatively unaware

Facilitative

4. Cathartic
Seeks to enable the client to discharge painful emotion, such as grief, fear or anger

5. Catalytic
Seeks to elicit self discovery, self-directed living, learning and problem solving in the client

6. Supportive
Seeks to affirm the worth and value of the client's person, qualities, attitudes or actions

What makes you say that?

A simple phrase, but excellent for getting clients to tell you what is behind their initial issue. Every adviser needs a repertoire of questions and phrases that dig under the surface. How many different way of saying "Tell me more" can you think of?

The Timeline

A way of helping a client look at where they want to be, is to review what they have and have not enjoyed up to now. You can draw a line representing their life, with their ages marked on it. Then ask them to mark out the highs (and lows, **if** you feel you can deal with any emotional response this may evoke), and to tell you what made those times special. You can ask them if they can see any patterns in the types of things they have enjoyed.

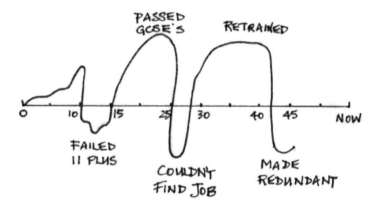

Build them up, Buttercup

It's easy to underestimate how difficult it can be for our clients to pick up the phone to ask us for information or advice or to walk through our door. Even though we know that seeking advice or guidance is wise and constructive, clients can feel overwhelmed, out of their comfort zone or as if they have failed by admitting they can't do it all for themselves. Sometimes we need to make an extra effort to build our clients' confidence, which may well have been battered by experiences far worse than coming to see us.

Aardvarc

Russell Webster (Webster, 2000) says "Ego food is in short supply but constant demand". He gives us the acronym AARDVARC to help us recall the things that we all need to motivate and engage us:

- Appreciation
- Acceptance
- Respect and Recognition
- Desire
- Value
- Approval
- Reassurance
- Compliments

Letting your client know they are accepted, valued, and that they have done well, even if it is only in coming to see you, will reap rewards in their confidence levels and their motivation to engage with you.

Find the Spark

Once we have started working with a client, it's easy to feel obligated to take a client all the way through an interview process, persevering even when it's not working. If it feels like pushing sand up a hill because the client is not responding as you would hope, take a step back and look for the spark that lights their lights. You may not find it if they are suffering from depression or are feeling low for another reason, but most folk have a subject that makes them animated and engaged. Return to exploring, and seek out what it is that they can respond to in a positive way, however small. This is the basic concept of motivational interviewing. There is a school of thought that says it is pointless to proceed until you find the spark, although whether or not you agree will to some extent depend on your job remit.

Once you find the spark, use the energy that comes with it to draw your client forward by linking it in some way to the purpose of your meeting. It can take a high degree of skill to do this, so don't be too cross with yourself if you don't get it right.

An experienced adviser was dealing with a very sullen, withdrawn client who participated minimally, but needed to do something about her education. The adviser managed to find out (and it wasn't easy!) that the girl loved horses, and became engaged and willing to talk about them. Every time the girl slumped in her chair and looked down, the adviser brought horses and stables into the conversation, and re-engaged her.

Hard work, but very effective.

Sales Talk

There are some tips we can glean from sales training that can occasionally have a place in advice and guidance. Sales people know that people buy only two things: solutions and benefits. There are times when we can use this concept to help clients plan their tactics to get what they need. If your client is trying to get a job, a house, or a place on a course, it can be helpful to think through what solutions or benefits they will bring the other party – and then make sure that that they stress these in any approach made. Not only will you increase your client's chance of success, but you will also bolster their self esteem by helping them discover positives they may not have considered.

What is your client's USP? That's Unique Selling Point, a phrase used by sales teams to differentiate their product from others on the market. If you have a client who is feeling they have nothing new to offer, you might want to help them figure out what is unique about their particular set of skills, experience and personality.

Sales professionals also have a distinctive take on rejection. They know that most customers say no several times before saying yes. So if they hear a No, they count it just a step on the way to a Yes, which is a very different perception to the usual doom and gloom resulting from rejection.

Expectancy

Victor Vroom (1999) believed that our expectations influence our motivation; the more likely we think something is to succeed, the more effort we will put into it, and vice versa. For example, if I want to go on holiday, and I expect that I should be able to find the time and the money, I will probably start looking at brochures in earnest. On the other hand, if I feel that I won't be able to get the time off work, or that I should spend my money on something more pressing, I doubt if I will get as far as the travel agents. The relevance to advice and guidance is that we may come up with action plans that our clients agree will lead them towards their goals, but they will be much more motivated if they expect their goals to be realised. What can we do to help our clients expect to see their plans achieved? Maybe we can help them picture a new future (using Visualisation, for example); we could use case studies of others who have reached a similar goal; or even just careful use of language could do the trick.

Take the client who did not succeed at school and is planning to get some basic qualifications at evening classes. He recognises that the qualifications will help his career progression, and intends to enrol but is not confident that he will pass, as history has taught him to expect failure. His adviser repositioned his expectancy by arranging a basic skills assessment and a discussion with a tutor. The tutor reassured him that previous students with his skills level had completed successfully, introduced him to teaching methods used and even showed him the learning environment. Once the client realised he was likely to succeed, his motivation and enthusiasm increased.

SMART Goals

Don't underestimate how motivating it can be to set goals. You may feel your client is not ready to face challenges, but even small steps can help us feel achievement and see progress - it's an upward spiral. Goals help us focus our time and energy, which in turn should make us more successful and productive by helping us control where we want to go in life. Some writers talk about a success mechanism inbuilt within all of us, but we can only kick start it if we have goals or targets to work towards.

SMART is an acronym used to define goals in various areas of work, for example training. People use the letters S M A R T to stand for different words, depending on the message they want to put across, although generally the words are similar.

To help clients set goals they have a chance of achieving, encourage them to make them:

S M A R T

Specific

- To touch-type at 30 wpm with under 5% errors (rather than the vague "to type faster")

Measurable

I will know I have achieved this when I can…
- type a letter of 120 words in four minutes,
- without looking at the keyboard,
- with no more than six mistakes.

**Appealing
Achievable
Attractive
Ambitious**

Is it something you really want to happen?
- I will get back into my favourite jeans

(more appealing than "I'll stop eating biscuits")

Realistic

Have you got (or can you get):
- the time?
- the money?
- the support?
- access to the right equipment?
- the aptitude (mental, physical)?

If there are any barriers, can they be overcome?

Timed

Give yourself a deadline for achieving the goal - a date for reviewing it to give yourself a pat on the back or maybe to readjust future goals.

Learning and Coaching

The dangers of Information Dumping have already been described, but almost every intervention requires us to teach our clients in some way, whether it is giving them information, or coaching them with the skills they need to progress, such as form filling, CV writing or interview techniques. How can we make sure the information we want to give them stays with them, rather than evaporating into the ether the minute they leave the room? Below are some general tips on how adults learn and take in information, followed by some frameworks and theories on coaching and learning.

How we learn

Giving advice and guidance is much easier if we have an understanding of how people learn, because when we are giving information or talking through options, we are wasting our breath if the client is not able to take it on board. Here is a random checklist to bear in mind:

- **Little by little** - The average brain will take in seven pieces of new information before it gives up. If clients are anxious, distracted, not used to the environment, or a myriad of other reasons, it could be a lot less.

- **Make connections** - Our brain will only take in what another person is saying if we can link it to something we already know, so it is essential that we find out what the client already knows, and watch that we don't use language or concepts they are unfamiliar with. If our brain cannot link what it is being said with anything already in its filing cabinets, it will delete it.

- **Bite size chunks** - Break it down into building blocks, starting with familiar ground for the client, make the links between the blocks obvious.

- **Repetition and Reinforcement** - If you reinforce information by repeating it (not necessarily verbatim), you stand a better chance of it being transferred from the clients short term to long term memory.

- **Understanding** - We learn best when we do not have to rely on memorising information or instructions. Understanding, not memory, leads to retention.

- **Relevance** - People learn effectively through activity at their own pace, with material that seems relevant to their daily lives.

- **Learning by Doing** - Most people learn more effectively when they participate in an activity, and are involved at every stage.

- **Feedback** should be given, or the individual will not know when they have learnt successfully.

- **Self directed** - People will be more motivated and engaged if the learning relates to goals that they have set themselves.

- **Individual differences** - People will have varying ability and different learning styles (see Learning Styles below). They will have been affected by their experience in many ways. You will need to adapt your approach to match the needs of the client.

Remember the wise words of Confucius:

I hear and I forget
I see and I remember
I do and I understand

GROW Model

John Whitmore (2002) pioneered the GROW model, which has been embraced by many organisations, particularly in the practice of coaching. In reality it is just a reflection of the advice/guidance process we have described, but it also demonstrates how the focus and common understanding of coaching has changed over the last twenty years. Traditionally, coaching involved passing on skills in a one-to-one setting, so if we are teaching a client how to answer interview questions or how to write a letter, it would fit the bill. Nowadays, coaching is still task focused, but puts the onus on the learner to identify the goals and methods of achieving them – you can see the overlap with advice and guidance.

Goal   What are your Goals? What outcome do you want?

Reality   What is the Reality? What is your present situation? Obstacles? Resources?

Options   What are your options? Alternatives? Advantages and disadvantages?

Will   What will you do? Which option do you choose? How will you get support?

Kolb's Learning Cycle

Kolb's Learning Cycle (Kolb, 1985) shows us the stages we need to go through for effective learning. Say we start by having an experience (for example, we attend an interview and don't get the job). Then we reflect on it (I wonder what went wrong? what could I have done differently? what do other people do?). After reflecting (and maybe researching by reading or asking people) we reach conclusions (it is advisable to find out more about the job in advance, to dress appropriately, to practise). We then plan to put these new ideas into practice next time. Kolb sees the process as a continuous spiral – this plan leads back to having the experience again to try out our plan, and then reflecting on how it worked this time, drawing new conclusions, and so on.

We may prefer to begin at any stage in the cycle, depending on our learning style. Some people will reflect and plan ahead before they try having an experience, for example. We all learn best by going through all four stages, but some people do not learn as much as they could because they do not enjoy one of the stages, and try to bypass it.

Concrete Experience
(doing / having an experience)

Active Experimentation
(planning / trying out what you have learned)

Reflective Observation
(reviewing / reflecting on the experience)

Abstract Conceptualisation
(concluding / learning from the experience)

Clients are not always aware that they have in fact learnt and moved forward. We often take them through the stages of the learning cycle by discussing their experiences with them, but it can be helpful at times to make this explicit, to help them see their progress.

Honey & Mumford's Learning Styles

Honey and Mumford developed Kolb's idea of the learning cycle by helping people to identify which of the four stages they prefer to operate in. Although there are a number of theories proposing different learning types, Honey and Mumford's Learning Styles (Honey & Mumford, 1992) tend to be the most commonly known. It is not as simple as falling into one of four boxes: most people are a mixture of two, three, or four. However, because people learn in different ways, we need to adapt our approach to suit the individual.

Honey & Mumford have produced a questionnaire to identify a person's preferred learning style(s). Even without doing the questionnaire, you may be able to help a client consider his preferred style and choose the right learning opportunities for him. Can you identify the learning styles of some of your clients from the way they respond to you?

On the following pages there is a brief description of the four learning styles. It is a worthwhile exercise to think how you can get the same point over to an individual with each of the different styles.

You can also think about what barriers each learning style might put in the way of a client trying to move forward, and how you can help them overcome them. You may need to encourage an activist to pause and think before rushing into the next activity. You can encourage a reflector to stop mulling it over and give it a try. A theorist can be encouraged to think outside the box, and not expect everything to be perfect. A pragmatist can be encouraged to look at alternative ways to approach a topic, to occasionally stand back and see the bigger picture.

Activists ...

... involve themselves fully and without bias in new experiences. They enjoy the here and now and are happy to be dominated by immediate experiences. They are open-minded, not sceptical, and this tends to make them enthusiastic about anything new. They can get bored if they do not have things to do.

Active Learners ...

... **like**:	... **do not like**:
• Working in the here and now rather than looking at what happened in the past, or at the wider implications	• A passive role (listening, reading, watching)
• Having a go, even if they get it wrong	• Working on their own (writing or homework assignments)
• Doing practical tasks	• Repetition (ie: practising over and over again)
• Short sessions with plenty of variety	• Having to follow instructions precisely
• To be in the limelight and to lead	• Following a methodical, structured programme with no uncertainties or challenges
• Having fun	

Reflectors ...

... like to stand back to ponder experiences and observe them from many different perspectives. They collect data, both first hand and from others, and prefer to chew it over thoroughly before coming to any conclusion. They tend to postpone reaching definitive conclusions or taking action for as long as possible.

Reflective Learners ...

... **like**:	... **do not like**:
• To think before they respond	• Being forced into the limelight, eg: role play
• To prepare thoroughly	• Having to take action without planning ahead
• To watch others and find out how things should be done, before trying for themselves	• Being expected to obey instructions without fully understanding the reasons
• To be given time to think over what has happened	• Being rushed
• Researching, going deeply into things	• Not having time to do a thorough job

Theorists ...

... think problems through in a step by step, logical way. They assimilate disparate facts into coherent theories. They tend to be perfectionists who will not rest easy until things are tidy and fit into their rational scheme. They like to analyse and synthesise. They are keen on basic assumptions, principles, theories, models and systems thinking. Their philosophy prizes rationality and logic. They do not like situations to be influenced by emotions and feelings.

Theoretical Learners ...

... like:

- To see the whole picture

- To form theories & see concepts and models

- Ideas to be presented logically

- Structure and clear objectives

- To be intellectually stretched

- To be able to discuss theories and concepts with other theorists

- To use systems and methodical approaches

- Analytical discussion

... do not like:

- Unstructured activities that have not been explained, where they is no apparent reason for doing them

- Using methods that seem unsound or unproven

- Being asked to do something without clear instructions or guidelines

- Working with fellow learners who appear less intelligent than them

- Studying topics that do not interest them

- Being asked to learn without the opportunity to research in depth

Pragmatists ...

... are the sort of people who return from management courses brimming with new ideas that they want to try out in the workplace. They like to get on with things and act quickly and confidently on ideas that attract them. They are essentially practical, down-to-earth people who like making realistic decisions and finding workable solutions. They respond to problems and opportunities as a challenge.

Pragmatic Learners ...

... **like**:

- Seeing how things will work in practice

- Trying out new ideas and solving problems

- An early opportunity to try out what they are learning

- Being advised by a coach or mentor who is expert in their field

- To watch demonstrations, to be given models and techniques

- To see the relevance of their learning to their work or their role

... **do not like**:

- Learning about things that are not relevant to their current situation or role

- Theory that does not appear to take into account the reality of the situation

- Being asked to do something without a clear explanation or guidelines

- Too much discussion around the point

- Political obstacles to an obvious solution

One Size Fits All?

Learning styles theory shows us that people are different – you knew that anyway! Knowing how to communicate effectively with different types, and how to vary your practice to suit each individual, is an art and a skill that you could keep on refining for ever. An approach that works well with one client can fail miserably with the next. Understanding the range of behavioural and learning styles can help you understand how best to relate to your client, and will also have significant impact on the actions that are appropriate for them. Knowing our own style is essential for advisers too, helping us see how we come across to others, and reminding us that not everyone views the world as we do, or feels comfortable (or uncomfortable) in the same situations.

It is outside the parameters of this book to give you a thorough grounding in the models and theories that abound to help us understand how people differ, and you have probably come across some yourself, but here is a swift canter through some of the most widely used. There are many others. Research those that interest you, and add to your toolbox an awareness of those you find most useful.

Personality Type Theories

We know that as long ago as the ancient Greeks, people have attempted to categorise personality types. Their four types, sanguine, melancholic, choleric and phlegmatic, can be compared with the poles of two dimensions suggested in more recent times by Freud and further developed by Hans Eysenck (Eysenck, 2006): Extrovert / Introvert and Neurotic / Stable.

Be warned - before you interpret these terms and make judgements based upon them, note that psychologists sometimes use terms that appear familiar, but often have meanings that may be different from their everyday use, so you may have to read further to gain sufficient understanding.

In Eysenck's model, the two dimensions intersect with each other, to produce the follow four possibilities:

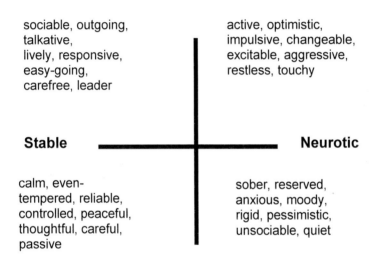

Extrovert

sociable, outgoing, talkative, lively, responsive, easy-going, carefree, leader

active, optimistic, impulsive, changeable, excitable, aggressive, restless, touchy

Stable

Neurotic

calm, even-tempered, reliable, controlled, peaceful, thoughtful, careful, passive

sober, reserved, anxious, moody, rigid, pessimistic, unsociable, quiet

Introvert

Jung / MBTI

Jung identified four ways in which people's thinking differs. Jungian theory is found in some psychometric instruments, such as the Myers Briggs Type Indicator, known as the MBTI (Briggs Myers with Myers, 1993) and the Jung Type Indicator, that are used to help people understand how they relate to and are perceived by others. The thought processes people use in one or other of 2 different ways are the four dichotomies:

Extraversion	or	Introversion
Sensing	or	iNtuition*
Thinking	or	Feeling
Judging	or	Perceiving

The theory is that we have a preference towards one or the other of each of these sets of opposites. Our four preferences, combined together, give a possible 16 different types. You may have heard of the combinations: ESTJ, INFP, INTJ, etc.

*NB: the letter N is used for Intuition because I has already been used for Introversion!

Tools such as MBTI help people discover their preference. It is important to note that the types depict a preference for acting in a certain way, not the forcefulness of the behaviour. There is a wealth of materials available to help you use and understand your MBTI results, such as understanding how to communicate most effectively with other types, how you may irritate others, strengths and weaknesses and areas for development.

Formal training is required for those who wish to administer MBTI and most other psychometric assessments. A brief description of the types follows, which may help you understand some of the many ways in which people feel and respond differently about things.

Extraversion………......…..…………Introversion

what interests us, what energises us

Extraverts are energised by the outer world of activity, people and things. They prefer to be around people. They like variety and action, pursuing a broad range of interests. They will think out loud, and often appear confident.	Introverts gain their energy from their inner world of reflections, feelings and ideas. They prefer interests that have depth, and they seek time on their own. They think before they speak. They appear more reserved.

Sensing……………..……….………………..iNtuition

how we take in information

Sensing types like information gained by using the five senses – they value what they can see, hear, touch, feel. They are practical, living in the here and now, preferring to use tried and tested skills and ways of doing things. They pay attention to details and are likely to be accurate.	Intuitive types like using 'sixth sense' and intuition, listening to their inner voice or gut reaction. They look to the future, liking change and rearranging life. Looking at the big picture, they enjoy learning new things, and doing things differently. They notice patterns and meanings written between the lines.

Thinking..Feeling

how we interpret and assess things

Thinking types base their decisions and problem-solving on logic and objective analysis. Truth and principles are important to them. They are fair, and may appear business- like and impersonal.	Feeling types base their decisions on their values, considering human needs, and seeking harmony. People are important to them, so they will be tactful and supportive. They are friendly and approachable.

Judging...Perceiving

how we respond to situations

Judging types prefer a planned, organised approach to life. They are more comfortable when things are decided and settled. They get things done and gain satisfaction from completion.	Perceiving types enjoy being spontaneous. They are flexible, and like to gather more information, enjoying the process more than completion. They like to keep their options open, so they may postpone decisions.

Belbin's Team Roles

Meredith Belbin (Belbin, 1993) is famous for his research into team types; he identified what kind of roles needed to be performed in teams, the theory being that for optimum performance, a team needs all the roles to be carried out. While this may not at first seem very relevant to advice and guidance, the fact that we all have a leaning towards one or more of the roles can shed light on the types of work roles that suit us. For example, you may be able to think of careers that will suit a Completer-Finisher, and different ones to suit a Plant or a Resource Investigator.

By highlighting our work style, the team role descriptions can also shed light on our personal style. This may help you understand how your client is responding to you, and how best to communicate with him. For example, a Plant may prefer to talk about ideas and concepts while an Implementer may prefer to discuss practicalities. The Shaper will want quick answers while the Resource Investigator may be happy to explore ideas.

Belbin devised a questionnaire to assess an individual's team type. Some of us will score across several of the roles, while others will have a strong preference for only one of them. The types are described below. Can you identify yourself, or some of your clients?

Implementer: **Conservative, dutiful, predictable**
- The practical organiser who turns ideas into manageable tasks
- Efficient administrator, producing schedules, charts and plans
- Methodical and can be relied on
- Prefers not to take the lead

The Co-ordinator	**Calm, self-confident**
	• Supervises the team and co-ordinates its work
	• Self-disciplined, maintains focus and balance
	• Works through others, by being a good judge of people and of situations
	• An effective communicator
	• Delegates well
	• May delegate too readily
The Shaper	**Energetic, outgoing, dynamic**
	• Has strong drive, passion, and motivation for the task
	• Likes to challenge and win, so can be seen as aggressive
	• Can be headstrong and impatient
	• Is a necessary spur to action
The Plant	**Individualistic, serious-minded, unorthodox**
	• Inventor and innovator - the source of original, sometimes radical, ideas
	• May not always be practical, can disregard protocol
	• Can tend to work independently
	• May not communicate well with those on a different wavelength
The Resource-Investigator	**Extroverted, enthusiastic, curious, communicative**
	• Extrovert, sociable and relaxed
	• Brings new contacts, ideas and developments to the team
	• Natural negotiator and networker
	• Sees possibilities
	• Not always practical or productive

The Monitor-Evaluator	**Sober, strategic, prudent**
	• Analyses ideas and sees the flaws in an argument
	• Shrewd and analytical, capable of a high level of critical thinking
	• Thinks things through and warns of possible pitfalls
	• Not likely to be inspiring as a leader

The Team Worker	**Socially orientated, diplomatic, gentle, sensitive**
	• Helps hold the team together, by being supportive to others
	• Listens, encourages, shows understanding
	• A peace-maker who dislikes friction
	• Can be indecisive

The Completer-Finisher	**Painstaking, orderly, conscientious, anxious**
	• The finisher who makes sure the team meets its deadlines
	• Pays great attention to detail and has a sense of urgency
	• Meticulous follow-through can irritate others
	• Dislikes carelessness and can be reluctant to delegate

The Specialist	**Professional, dedicated, expert**
	• Takes a pride in acquiring specialist skills and knowledge
	• Provides essential expertise
	• Committed and single minded
	• May not be interested in other viewpoints
	• Maintains high standards in own field

Holland's Career Types

J.R. Holland (Holland, 1973) found that people tend to choose and be happy and successful in careers and jobs that match their personalities and interests. He identified six personality types and suggested types of careers likely to suit them:

- *Realistic* people usually enjoy practical activities and prefer to get things done rather than talk about them. Their preferred occupations may be in fields such as engineering, manufacturing, construction, surveying, farming, or transport. They may prefer to focus on a task, and on achieving an objective.

- *Investigative* people enjoy exploring and investigating why or how things occur or work. They take an intellectual, theoretical approach to tasks, and like to go deeply into a topic rather than just skim the surface. They usually have the tenacity and concentration to see a job through to its conclusion. Their work could be in scientific, technical or social research or information professions.

- *Artistic* people enjoy imaginative or creative activities. It is possible to show a high interest in this type of work without being an artist. Such people often take a creative approach to their work, needing to be able to produce something with pride, and to see a finished product for which they feel ownership. They may be sensitive to feelings, culture and the natural world.

- *Social* people want to help and care for others and to improve their lives. Their work could be in social services, youth and community development, teaching, nursing, therapies, care of elderly or handicapped people, child care. They like to build and maintain relationships and probably prefer to work directly with individuals.

- *Enterprising* people enjoy activities which give them the opportunity to persuade or organise other people. They tackle problems with energy and enthusiasm. Their preferred work may be in fields such as management, sales work, public relations and marketing.

- *Conventional* people like to plan and organise. They enjoy clerical and administrative activities like checking information or calculating figures. Often well organised and tidy minded people, their work could be in finance and accountancy, quality assurance, project planning, library and information work, computing or transport administration.

The relationship between these six career types can be represented by a diagram: each type will share most characteristics with those adjacent to it on the hexagon, tending to have least in common with those furthest away.

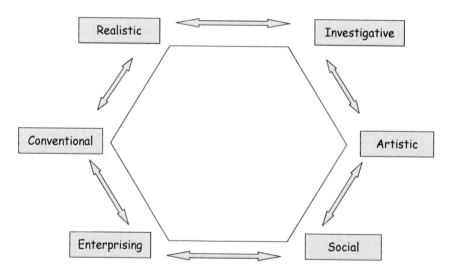

While this career matching approach to career guidance is now seen as just one of many ways to help people work out who they are and where they want to be, many clients do find it helpful in making sense of what feels right for them.

NLP Categories

NLP (Neuro linguistic programming) was devised in the 1970's by Richard Bandler and colleagues (Bandler and Grinder, 1979). It provides a complex set of tools and theories that help us understand communication. NLP has identified three 'mind methods': Visual, Auditory and Kinaesthetic. If you can recognise which one your client is using, the theory is that you can adapt your language to make it more relevant and meaningful to them. We all use all three modes to some degree, so it is not as simple as categorising everyone into the three boxes, but looking for the dominant method being used can help us understand why we 'hit it off' with some folk more than others.

There are many books and training courses that you can access if you want to know more about NLP, in addition to the original text listed in the bibliography.

The Visual Person

The theory suggests you can identify them by their use of visual language, e.g. "I see what you mean..." "The big picture is..." "I can visualise...". They are often quick thinkers and talkers, as they put their vision into words. They can be expressive, sometimes creative.

They need to see and position facts and ideas in space. Diagrams and pictures will help them understand what you are trying to explain. They will switch off if you just talk to them.

The Auditory Person

You may recognise this type of person by phrases like "I hear what you are saying...." "that sounds good for me...". They tend to speak at a more normal pace than the Visuals, their voices are more measured, they choose words more carefully. They will be able to take in more verbal information, spoken and probably also written.

The Kinaesthetic Person

Kinaesthetics major on their feelings, they may be more interested in interpreting their gut reaction than talking to you. They may use metaphors from the physical world, or talk about being "being in touch". They may take longer to put their ideas and feelings into words; they may reply by shrugging or other non verbal responses rather than speaking, and put deep breaths between sentences.

They may take longer to process spoken information or respond to questions. If you are aware of this, you will not be offended, nor interpret their silence as lack of interest or of intelligence. You can give them longer to answer your questions.

They may prefer to work out their ideas through a practical activity, such as a card sort or a manual tool like the Rickter Scale. They may discover their preferences more easily from active involvement such as role play or work experience rather than from discussion and questionnaires.

Kelly's Personal Construct Theory

George Kelly (Kelly, 1991) provides a method for identifying the unique way in which each of us sees the world. This can help you understand the world from the client's point of view, and therefore support him in identifying what is important to him when he is making decisions. We cannot provide you with a list of constructs, because unlike type theories or matching models, the whole point is that they are determined by each individual, and unique to that person.

A number of careers advisers have used Kelly's basic principle to devise this exercise to discover a client's personal constructs in relation to career choice: Take about eight blank cards (or fold an A4 sheet in half three times and tear along the folds into eight pieces). On each, write a job title. To help you get a range of titles, try to include some you feel positive about and others you feel negative towards, for example:

| *A job you would be able to do* | *A job you would hate to do* | *A job someone else has suggested* | *A job you could not do* | *A job you'd love to do* |

...etc.

Turn the cards face down and pick up three of them.

Turn the three over and read them. Divide them into a group of 2 and a group of 1, with the two most similar together, and the most different one on its own.

Now try to describe the basis for your decision. Say:

> ➤ These two jobs are .... and the other one isn't.

Then put the three cards back face down, shuffle them all and select another three.

Repeat the exercise 5 or 6 times, each time noting down what makes the two similar ones different from the third one.

The words you have written probably reveal what is important to you about jobs, and the criteria against which you will make your decisions.

As an example, supposing you and I choose the same three jobs to look at:

Solicitor	Nurse	Careers Adviser

I might say that Solicitor and Careers Adviser were the same, and Nurse different. My rationale might be that Solicitors and Careers Advisers provide solutions through discussion and information, and they work in an office, whereas a Nurse's role is more practical, hands on, physically touching patients, more active, and based in a hospital.

You might say Nurse and Careers Adviser were the same, and Solicitor different. The reason for your choice might be that Nurses and Careers Advisers work in the public sector and their main purpose is to help people, whereas a Solicitor works in the private sector and works for profit.

A third person might say that Nurses and Solicitors are the same because they are well known professions, whereas Careers Advisers are less well known with less obvious career progression routes.

Whether or not any of these interpretations of the work of solicitors, nurses and careers advisers are correct or well informed is beside the point. The fact is that each of us has given some vital indicators about what we feel is important about careers. For one it is whether or not they are "helping people, non-profit making", for another it is whether they are "working with information, in an office environment" or "active, hands-on", for another it is "a well known profession with clear entry and progression routes".

As an adviser, we may or may not share these preferences or values, but we need to know what our client's values are, so that we can help them make their choices on the basis of their own values, not ours.

Having identified an individual's personal constructs, you can make each one into a scale for them. (See earlier in this section: Scales). Then you can ask them where on the scale their perfect job would be. Eg:

| 1 | 2 | 3 | 4 | 5 | 6 | 7 | 8 | 9 | 10 |

helping people ------------------------------------X--------------profit making

| 1 | 2 | 3 | 4 | 5 | 6 | 7' | 8 | 9 | 10 |

well known profession ----X---------------------------------------little known

| 1 | 2 | 3 | 4 | 5 | 6 | 7 | 8 | 9 | 10 |

information, paperwork -------------------X------------- hands-on, practical

etc.

Super's Rainbow – his Life Span Life Space Theory

Donald Super (Super, 1985) gave us two principal theories about how people make choices about careers. The first is his developmental theory, of particular use in helping us understand how young people go through several increasingly realistic phases as they consider careers in relation to who they feel they are (their self-concept). The second is his Life Span Life Space Theory which suggests that we all act out our lives in nine different "theatres" or arenas, playing a different role in each. The roles are:

Child   *Spouse*   *Worker*   *Leisurite*
Student   *Homemaker*   *Parent*   *Pensioner*

We all perform in several of the arenas at any one time and juggle the various roles, allocating various amounts of time and attention to each. He presents these in the form of a rainbow with nine strands, one for each role.

To help a client see what they are focusing on at present, and how their focus may be different from how it was five years ago, or how it could be in ten years' time, you can show the visual image of the rainbow and ask them to tell you which role is most important to them at the moment.

Seeing our lives as a rainbow of different roles may help to explain why a client is making what seem on the face of it to be making odd choices. If I have built a successful career and have the option of climbing still higher, but my wife has become ill and I want to spend more time with her, I can be helped to understand the conflict this is causing and why I am no longer interested in my career. If I feel disappointed that I no longer have time to contribute to the community, nor to study or have fun as I used to, the Rainbow can help me to see that since those days, I have taken on perhaps three new roles: spouse, home-maker and parent. I realise that I would have to spread myself too thinly to try and perform in so many roles at one time. I can also see that a time will come when my parenting role may be less time-consuming, or that maybe I need to make the hard decision to put one of the roles on the back burner for a while, to give myself a breather.

This theory shows clients how to take back control of their lives, and prioritise between the roles. The title of the book "Build your own Rainbow" (Hopson and Scally, 1999) is suggesting just this – it is our own rainbow, and we can decide how it is made up.

Are you my Mother?

Transactional Analysis (TA) looks at roles in a different way, helping to explain a danger that can creep up on us in our interactions with clients (and others). This is the theory that says we have three modes of operation open to us when we are communicating: parent, child and adult.

- **Parent behaviour** provides discipline and protection, as you would for a young child. Parents can be critical (stemming from feelings of what is proper and right) or nurturing (wanting to help and protect the other person from difficulties or dangers that face them).

- **Child behaviour** is spontaneous and led by feelings. Child behaviour can be subdivided into **natural child** (impulsive, playful, fearful, self-indulgent, rebellious) and **adaptive child**, where impulses are toned down to make them more acceptable to others (eg teasing, whining, manipulating).

- **Adult behaviour** is characterised by logic and reason. It stems from thinking, not feeling. Adult behaviour is rational, gathering and evaluating information before using it to make realistic choices.

For professional working relationships the preferred communication is adult to adult. However, sometimes people have a tendency to slip into parent or child mode, often as a result of childhood experience or upbringing. Think of the possible combinations of interaction in your work. There will be times when you are aware that your feelings are not from the appropriate mode of operation, or you recognise that the client is not responding as you expected.

If we have a client that is unconsciously acting in the role of child, it is very easy to respond as a parent or school teacher would. Is that your role? We would suggest that in the role of adviser we are either working with adults or we are preparing young people to enter the adult world. Our aim is to empower them to take care of themselves. Accepting the role of parent that the client has given us will be a natural response, but it is not appropriate for the situation. We should be aiming to shift the relationship to one between two adults. As we try to do this, responding as an adult to a client who is operating as a child, it may go against the grain and feel uncomfortable, but it is in the client's interest (and yours as adviser – you don't really want to be their parent) to persevere and explore ways of shifting the client into acting as an adult. Eric Berne (Berne, 1964) devised and Thomas Harris (Harris, 1995) popularised Transactional Analysis.

The diagram on the next page can help us understand how interactions might start, and how we might try to introduce changes so that they become more productive, enabling the client to take ownership of their situation:

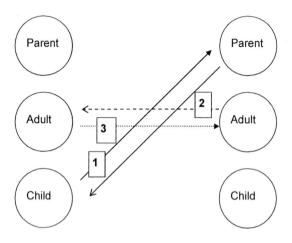

The arrows show the transactions…

1. Client addresses adviser in child mode
   Adviser responds in parent mode

2. Adviser decides to alter the relationship and respond in adult mode

3. Client responds in adult mode

An example:

Child Client: "There's nothing I can do, no one will give me a job. There's no point trying any more."

Nurturing Parent Adviser: "You poor thing, don't worry, I'll sort it out for you."

Critical Parent Adviser: "Well maybe if you made more effort, you'd have more success."

Child Adviser: "I agree. It's not fair. I blame the government. It's not our fault if we give up."

Adult Adviser: "I can see you're feeling really down. Let's look at what you've tried so far, and explore what you can do to improve your chances."

Another example:

Child Client: "My parents will never agree to it. Would you talk to them, they'd listen to you?"

Adult Adviser: "No, I think you should talk to them, but I can help you prepare what you will say and how you will approach them, and you can come back and see me afterwards to tell me how it went. What do you think of that?"

PART 4
FURTHER DEVELOPMENT AND SUPPORT

Our aim with this book has been to give you a basic structure on which to build your one-to-one advice and guidance work. If you already have all the qualifications you need, but enjoyed reviewing your practice and picking up some new ideas, you can look in the bibliography and resources list for more in-depth reading on the methods and techniques listed in the Toolkit.

If you are quite new to advice and guidance work, you may now want to build on what you have learned and get qualifications that will move your career forward. This section lists the main qualifications and courses available in the UK for advisers, guidance practitioners, coaches and mentors.

Qualifications and training programmes

Change is always with us and the world of qualifications is no exception. In England, Wales and Northern Ireland, NVQs are in many cases being replaced by "vocationally related qualifications" (VRQs) with learning outcomes that require a balance of practical skills and theory. A new suite of VRQs has been designed specifically for the career guidance sector, to run alongside the generic Advice and Guidance qualifications that can suit all advisers. Similar frameworks exist in Scotland and the Republic of Ireland.

The growth of coaching has continued and with it a movement to ensure the quality of coaches through qualifications and professional bodies. This has brought a number of new qualifications in coaching and mentoring, developed by professional bodies and, increasingly, universities.

The Register of Career Development Professionals

A major change in the career advice and guidance sector is the coming together in 2012 of four professional bodies to form the Career Development Institute (CDI) which has set up a Register of Career Development Professionals, with admission based on the practitioner's qualifications, job role and commitment to its ethical code and continuing professional development.

Currently the qualifications that are specified as meeting the requirement for immediate entry to the Register of Career Development Professionals are:

- Qualification in Career Guidance (QCG)
- Qualification in Career Guidance and Development (Scotland) (QCGD)

These qualifications are awarded by the Institute of Career Guidance (ICG - one of the four constituent bodies forming the CDI). The ICG (www.icg-uk.org) states that QCG and QCGD will equip you to find employment as a guidance practitioner in the statutory services and also in further and higher education careers advisory services, the voluntary sector and a growing private sector.

The QCG is available at a number of universities across the UK, and the QCGD at certain universities in Scotland (www.icg-uk.org lists these course centres). They are available as a one-year full time or two year part time course with distance learning options available in some cases. For entry, you will need to demonstrate that you can cope with postgraduate level study but you need not necessarily have a first degree.

- Diploma in Career Guidance (Parts 1 and 2)
- Diploma in Career Guidance combined with the NVQ Level 4 in Guidance
- Postgraduate Diploma in Career Development and Coaching Studies or in Career Education, Information and Guidance in Higher Education (University of Warwick)

Most Postgraduate Diplomas include the QCG/QCGD. They are run by the universities listed on the ICG website listed above and offer a combination of theory and work placements. Part 2 is completed while working in a career guidance position and usually involves completion of the Institute of Career Guidance Certificate in Professional Practice.

- QCF Level 6 Diploma in Career Guidance and Development

This qualification, launched in 2010, has been primarily designed for people who already work in the career guidance sector and want to gain accreditation for their existing skills and, in addition, increase their skills and knowledge. There are no specific entry requirements, but in order to gain the qualification you have to show you meet the assessment criteria which include a combination of theoretical knowledge, factual knowledge and competence in the workplace. There is no specified time limit for the achievement of this qualification other than the expiry dates for entry and certification.

There are further qualifications that are acceptable for membership of the Register if supplemented by specified units of the Level 6 Diploma. There is also an alternative route via a competency framework for people with a degree or postgraduate qualification in any subject. Please note that as the CDI develops, all these requirements will continue to be reviewed and will always be liable to change, therefore it is important to check up to date details of all routes on the website www.cparegister.org.

Other Qualifications and Courses

Before we list some of the courses available to you, a word about the differences between them.

Qualifications – some courses do not lead to a qualification, but may still be very valuable to you. You might find a short one-day or half-day course run by your employer, or by a local college or other organisation, which offers the exact training you are looking for.

Accredited Qualifications

In England, Wales and Northern Ireland, QCF (the Qualifications and Credit Framework) is the national system which assures you a qualification meets certain accepted standards and will provide a pathway on to further qualifications if you want them. Universities offer their own qualifications and these are allocated a level in the Framework for Higher Education Qualifications (FHEQ). SQCF is the framework for all Scottish qualifications and the Republic of Ireland also has a qualifications framework.

Levels

The Frameworks specify the level of each course. QCF has a total of 9 levels from Entry Level through Level 1 to Level 8. FHEQ qualifications range from level 4 (Certificate of Higher Education) to level 8 (Doctoral Degree). Honours degrees are at level 6. Postgraduate Diplomas and Masters degrees are at level 7. In Scotland, SQCF qualifications are divided into 12 levels, including higher education qualifications up to Doctorate level.

Award, Certificate or Diploma?

QCF qualifications at each level may be an Award, a Certificate or a Diploma, depending on the number of credits achieved. Awards are smallest (therefore probably shortest), with the least number of credits possible, and Diplomas the largest. You will learn more on a Diploma course than on an Award or Certificate, but the learning will all be at the same level of difficulty and depth.

Professional bodies also offer qualifications that are recognised within the profession.

Value for Money?

If the course you choose has been accredited by a nationally recognised organisation, you have some indication as to its quality and standing, although it is still advisable to gather information about it and consider whether it is worth the fee you will spend on it. This is all the more important for a course that has not been accredited.

Reflective Practice

Change is not only imposed by government, it also comes from the grass roots. New ideas and methods are developed, both by academics and by practitioners. If you are a professional, you will be a reflective practitioner, keeping your eyes and ears (and your mind) open. You will take time to review how well your methods are working, and to explore new ideas that may help you improve your service to clients.

At the end of this chapter (p195) we've included a Personal Development Plan, that you can use to record your reflections and plan the best way to develop and increase your skills. You can also buy a more in-depth Reflective Diary (Bassot, 2012) for students and trainees that guides you through up to two years of self-reflection exercises.

The courses

Most of the courses you will find listed here are those accredited in England, Wales and Northern Ireland. We hope the range of options listed will give people outside this area a basis to search for similar courses in their own country.

If you are not already working as an adviser, guidance practitioner, coach or mentor

You may want to find a course that will give you a taste of the skills needed. Courses in basic listening and counselling skills may be available at your local college. If you know the college, search their website, get a prospectus or ring them for information.

Some courses will give you a taste and provide you with a qualification. Here are some of the qualifications you can look for in your local area. To search, contact the awarding body/organisation that offers them (listed in brackets beside each qualification) or use the National Careers Service website course search.

Level 1
- Information, Advice or Guidance *(AIM, NOCN, Open Awards)*

Level 2
- Information, Advice or Guidance *(AIM, NOCN, Open Awards)*
- Counselling Skills and/or Concepts *(ABC, AQA, Ascentis, CPCAB, Edexcel, ITEC, NCFE)*
- Introduction to Life Coaching Skills *(Edexcel BTEC)*

Level 3
- Counselling Studies, Skills and Theory (ABC, AQA, Ascentis, CPCAB, Edexcel, ITEC, NCFE)

There are QCF and other courses in Counselling at higher levels, but these are not included here as we are focusing on the skills that you will need for Advice, Guidance, Coaching and Mentoring. For more information, look on the website of the British Association of Counselling and Psychotherapy (www.bacp.co.uk).

Degrees and Postgraduate Courses

There are some first degrees that give an insight and basic preparation for advice, guidance, coaching and mentoring work, and the best way to find them is to search on the UCAS website (www.ucas.ac.uk) for key words: Advice work; Guidance; Counselling; Psychology; Childhood studies; Youth studies.

The postgraduate courses that provide a direct route into career guidance work are the Postgraduate Diplomas in Career Guidance listed above as approved by the Career Development Institute.

If you want to keep your options more open, you can search on the Prospects website (www.prospects.ac.uk) for Masters Courses in: Coaching; Mentoring; Counselling; Psychology; Career

Management; Guidance. You will find a wide choice of courses on offer, including the Masters courses in Guidance which you will find listed on the ICG website (www.icg-uk.org). If you are looking to work in the private and corporate sector, there is some evidence that large companies and outplacement firms prefer postgraduate study of coaching or psychology, with business experience at a senior level.

Volunteering

As an alternative to enrolling on a course, you may decide to join a specialist agency as a volunteer and receive training from them. Some are well known for the quality of their training, including Citizen's Advice Bureau, Relate and the Samaritans. Be aware that each would expect a mature outlook and considerable commitment from their volunteers. In some schools and colleges, peer support schemes operate, where student peer mentors would receive some basic training in empathy, listening and handling difficult situations, as well as how to refer clients to specialist help.

Do you already work with clients in an organisation that provides information, advice, guidance and/or support to clients?

If so, you can work towards a vocationally related qualification, which generally requires you to be working in a position that allows you to practise and be assessed in the skills you are learning. Here are the names of a few qualifications available in 2013 within the QCF. Your employer may already know of a centre that offers the course you want, and for more information about the course and a list of centres that offer it, you can:
- search using your preferred search engine
- contact one of the organisations that award the qualification (listed in brackets after each qualification)

Information, Advice and/or Guidance

Level 2
- Information, Advice or Guidance *(NOCN)*

Level 3
- Advice and Guidance *(OCR, City & Guilds, Edexcel, EDI, NCFE, Proqual)*
- Information, Advice or Guidance *(NOCN)*

Level 4
- Advice and Guidance *(OCR, City & Guilds, Edexcel, EDI, NCFE, Proqual)*

Career Advice and Guidance

Level 3
- Supporting Clients to Overcome Barriers to Learning and Work *(OCR, AIM)*
- Information and Advice for Supporting Learner Progression *(AIM, Open Awards)*
- Employment Related Services (*Agored Cymru in Wales*) *(EDI, OCR)*

Level 4
- Career Information and Advice *(OCR, City & Guilds, SFEDI)*
- Employment Related Services (*Agored Cymru in Wales*) *(EDI)*

Level 6
- Career Guidance and Development *(City & Guilds, OCR, SFEDI)*

Legal Advice

Level 2
- Supporting Legal Advice Provision *(OCR, Proqual)*

Level 3
- Providing Initial Legal Information and Advice *(OCR, Proqual)*

Level 4
- Providing Specialist Legal Advice *(Proqual)*

Level 5
- Providing Specialist Advice to Young People on their Rights under the Law *(Proqual)*
  Providing Legal Advice to Older People *(Proqual)*

Coaching and Mentoring

Level 1 and Level 2
- Mentoring *(NCFE)* and Peer Mentoring *(OCNLR, Edexcel BTEC)*

Level 3
- Coaching (focuses on coaching in the workplace *(City & Guilds, ILM)*
- Coaching and Mentoring *(City & Guilds, CMI, ILM)*
- Life Coaching Studies *(CPCAB)*
- Life Coaching Skills and Practice *(Edexcel BTEC)*

Level 4
- Coaching for Learning (14-19s) *(Agored Cymru)*
- Providing Skills Advice to Business *(SFEDI)*

Level 5
- Management Coaching and Mentoring *(CMI, ILM)*

Level 7
- Leadership Coaching and Mentoring *(CMI)*
- Executive Coaching and Mentoring *(ILM)*

As change is always with us, please be aware that organisations may change their names or merge. This information has been taken from the website www.ofqual.gov.uk in January 2013.
- For the latest picture in England, Wales or Northern Ireland, you can visit the Ofqual Register of Regulated Qualifications.
- If in Scotland, please refer to www.sqcf.org.uk or www.sqa.org.uk.
- For qualifications in the Republic of Ireland, see www.nfq.ie.
Remember also, that just because a qualification exists, it does not mean that any provider is offering it at this time, so when you contact the awarding organisation, ask for a list of providers currently delivering the qualification.

Values and Ethics

You will have noticed we mention values at various points throughout this book. We ask you to be clear about your own values and we point out how every client's values guide his choices and decisions.

We believe that everyone reading this book values helping and supporting others, and is aiming to be client-centred in their work. The purpose of their job is primarily to help individual clients, rather than to make money for their organisation (although remaining in profit is important, or you couldn't be there for your clients).

The nature of one-to-one work with clients means we are unsupervised by anyone. We ask clients to reveal their hopes and fears to us. We help them shape their goals for the future. There is the potential to do damage.

Most helping professions have a Code of Ethics to help members keep their practice client-centred and to protect individuals against harm. Both the National Association of Educational Guidance for Adults and the Institute of Career Guidance have a Code of Practice that members are required to work within. The new Career Development Institute is currently developing its Code of Ethics which is likely to mirror the existing bodies' ethical codes in focusing on the principles of:

- **Impartiality**
- **Confidentiality**, making it clear if, where and when confidentiality cannot be maintained
- **Client-Centred**, based on the client's needs and acting in his/her best interest
- **Equality** and **Diversity**
- **Respect** for each client's beliefs, values, dignity, privacy and their right to make independent choices and take responsibility for those choices and their consequences
- **Maintaining professional competence** in reviewing and updating skills and knowledge

If you work to these principles, you will be offering professional and ethical client-centred, impartial advice, guidance and support.

My Interview Skills Review and Personal Development Plan

Date		
Trigger	What went wrong? What would have been better?	
Development need	What competence do you need to develop further?	
Ideas	How might you develop this competence?	
Action plan	What action will you take and when?	
Goal (SMART)	What result would you like to see from this action?	
Target date	Set a target date to evaluate	
Evaluation	Leave blank for progress review on target date.	

Please read the Postscript

We would like to hear from you.

As we said in the beginning, there is no way a practical handbook such as this can include every tool of the trade. We chose those that we have tried and tested, but there may be many others that you have found useful. There may also be topics that you wished we had covered in more depth or from a different angle, or questions that you would like answered. Please let us know your thoughts, comments, ideas and questions. We will bear them in mind for future updates.

Our Other Books

We have produced a companion volume, **"The Groupwork Toolkit"** (ISBN 978-0-9559680-1-3) because we were aware that many advisers and coaches are being asked to work with groups, rather than individual clients. Please do check it out if this applies to you. It contains strategies, activities and sample session plans, as well as advice on how to put together a great group session.

"**The Job Interview Toolkit**" (ISBN 978-0-9559680-2-0) followed, based on Ann's highly successful "Do Better in Job Interviews" workshops. Here you will find many practical, accessible exercises that can be used with either individual clients or groups, using the simple TAPAS framework.

Julie has also written **"Face to Face in the Workplace"** (ISBN 978-0-9559680-3-7), an A-Z guide for busy line managers to help them get the best out of all their one to one conversations. It has 26 step by step frameworks covering all the discussions managers are involved in, from appraisals to supervisory meetings.

We would be happy to hear your feedback on any of our books.

Julie Cooper and Ann Reynolds
info@careertrain.net / www.careertrain.net

BIBLIOGRAPHY AND RESOURCES

Ali, Lynda and Graham, Barbara, 1996, *The Counselling Approach to Careers Guidance,* Hove, Routledge.

Bandler, Richard & Grinder, John, 1979, *Frogs into Princes: Neuro Linguistic Programming,* Real People Press.

Bassot, Barbara, 2012, *The Reflective Diary*, Matador, Troubadour Publishing Ltd, Leicestershire

Bedford, Tol, 1982, *Vocational Guidance Interviews Explored,* London, Careers Service Branch, Department of Employment.

Belbin, R. Meredith, 1993, *Management Teams: Why they succeed or fail,* 2nd ed, Butterworth-Heinemann.

Berne, Eric, 1964, *Games people play: the psychology of human relationships*, New York, Grove Press.

Beven, P, 1995 "Using Personal Construct Theory in Careers Education and Guidance" in *Careers Education and Guidance, NACGT*, Feb 1995.

Bimrose, J., Barnes, S-A., Hughes, D. and Orton, M. (2004) *What is Effective Guidance? Evidence from Longitudinal Case Studies in England,* DfES/Warwick Institute for Employment Research.

Bimrose, J., Barnes, S-A., and Hughes, D. (2005) *Effective Guidance One Year On: Evidence From Longitudinal Case Studies in England,* DfES/Warwick Institute for Employment Research.

Bimrose, J., Barnes, S-A., and Hughes, D. (2006) *Developing Career Trajectories in England: The Role of Effective Guidance,* DfES/Warwick Institute for Employment Research.

Briggs Myers, Isabel with Myers, Peter B, 1980, *Gifts Differing: understanding personality type,* Palo Alto, Ca, USA, Consulting Psychologists Press.

Buzan, Tony, 2002, *How to mindmap: the thinking tool that will change your life,* Harper Collins Publishers Ltd.

Cattell, Raymond B, Cattell, Karen S and Heather E P, *16PF5 (5th edition),* Oxford, UK: OPP Ltd (training is required to purchase and administer this instrument).

De Bono, Edward, 1994, *Edward De Bono's Thinking Course,* BBC Books.

De Bono, Edward, 2000, *Six Thinking Hats 2nd ed,* London: Penguin.

Department for Education and Skills, 2003, *Information, Advice and Guidance for Adults – Towards a National Policy Framework: Discussion Document, London,* DfES.

Department for Education and Skills (DfES)/Learning and Skills Council (LSC)/Ufl, 2003, *Information, Advice and Guidance for Adults:The National Policy Framework and Action Plan,* London, Learning and Skills Council.

Egan, Gerard, 1994, *The Skilled Helper: a problem management approach to helping,* 5th ed, California USA: Wadsworth.

Eysenck, Hans J., 2006, *The Biological Basis of Personality* (Chapter 2, esp. page 38), Piscataway, NJ, Transaction Publishers.

Harris, Thomas,1995, *I'm OK, You're OK,* Arrow Books.

Heron, John, 1989, *Six Category Intervention Analysis,* Human potential Resource Group, University of Surrey

Holland, John L, 1973, *Making Vocational Choices: a theory of careers,* Englewood Cliffs, NJ, USA, Prentice-Hall.

Honey Peter, 1988, *Improve your People Skills,* London: Institute of Personnel Management.

Honey Peter and Mumford Alan, 1992, *The Manual of Learning Styles*, Maidenhead: Peter Honey Publications Ltd.

Hopson, Barry and Scally, Mike, 1999, *Build Your Own Rainbow: a lifeskills workbook for career and life management*, Cirencester, UK: Management Books 2000 Ltd.

Instone, Ayd, *Who do you think you are?* http://www.aydinstone.com/article-18.html (09/01/2013)

Jolley, Rosemary, 2001, *Developing Adult Guidance Skills*, Cambridge: National Extension College.

Kelly, George A, 1991, *The Psychology of Personal Constructs, vol 1 A Theory of Personality*, 3rd ed. London, Routledge.

Kidd, Jennifer M, 2006, *Understanding Career Counselling: Theory, Research and Practice,* London, Sage Publications Ltd.

Kolb, David A, 1985, *Experiential Learning: experience as the source of learning and development,* Englewood Cliffs, NJ, USA: Prentice-Hall.

Kubler-Ross, Elisabeth, 1997 reprint, *On Death and Dying,* Scribner.

Learning and Skills Council, 2004, *Coherent Information, Advice and Guidance (IAG) Services for Adults,* Learning and Skills Council.

Maslow, Abraham Harold, 1987, *Motivation and Personality*, 3rd (revised) edition, Harper and Row, New York.

Mehrabian, Albert, 1971, *Silent Messages,* Wadsworth Publishing.

Myers, Isabel and Briggs, Katharine C, *MBTI (Myers Briggs Type Indicator),* Oxford, UK: OPP Ltd (training is required to purchase and administer this instrument).

Myers, Isabel Briggs with Myers, Peter B, 1993, *Gifts Differing,* CPP Books, California.

NAEGA (2003), *The Challenge of Change: developing educational guidance for adults*, (National Association of Educational Guidance for Adults (NAEGA).

Nelson Jones, Richard, 2000, *Introduction to Counselling Skills,* London: Sage Publications.

Offer, M, 1995 "Personal Construct Theory – a complete programme for CEG?" in *Careers Education and Guidance journal of the NACGT*, Oct 1995.

Reid, H, 2006, Constructing the Future: Transforming Career Guidance, *Constructing the Future: Transforming Career Guidance, p 7-19*, Institute of Career Guidance.

Rickter Scale® - more information from www.rickterscale.com

Robbins, Anthony, 1997, *Unlimited Power: the new science of personal achievement,* Free Press.

Rogers, Carl R., 1967, *On Becoming a Person: A Psychotherapist's View of Psychotherapy,* 2nd ed., London, Constable and Company Ltd.

Super, Donald, 1985, *New Dimensions in Adult Vocational and Career Counseling,* Ohio State University Center on Education.

Vroom, Victor, 1999 2nd ed, *Management and Motivation,* Penguin UK.

Webster, Russell, 2000, *Super Communication the NLP Way,* David Grant Publishing Ltd

Whitmore, John, 2002, 3rd ed, *Coaching for Performance,* Nicholas Brealey Publishing.

INDEX

Harris, Thomas, 181, 198
Helicopter vision, 126
Heron, John, 134, 148, 198
Holland, John, 26, 78, 90, 172, 198
Honey, Peter, 123, 198
Honey, Peter and Mumford, Alan, 159, 199

IAG or Information, Advice and Guidance, 5, 14, 34, 71
ICG (Institute of Career Guidance), 34, 186
Immediacy, 27, 83, 135
Impartial, impartiality, 30, 54, 93
Information, 36, 54-59, 71-72
Institute of Career Guidance (ICG), 34, 186
Instone, Ayd, 140, 199
Interest inventories, assessments or questionnaires, 78

Jolley, Rosemary, 65, 102, 107-108, 199
Jung, Carl, 166

Kelly, George, 90, 176, 199
Kolb, David, 157, 159, 199
Kubler Ross, Elizabeth, 129, 199

Language, 21, 55-56, 80, 126, 147, 153, 155, 174
Lateral thinking, 119, 144
Learning and Coaching, 155-156
Learning and Work, 5, 65, 71, 73, 129, 146
Learning cycle, 157-159
Learning styles, 159-163
Level 6 Diploma in Career Guidance and Development, 186
Lifeline, 77
Life span life space theory, 179
Limitations, 35, 101, 190 (*see also* Boundaries)
Listening, 8, 38-48